SNOW, GLASS, APPLES™

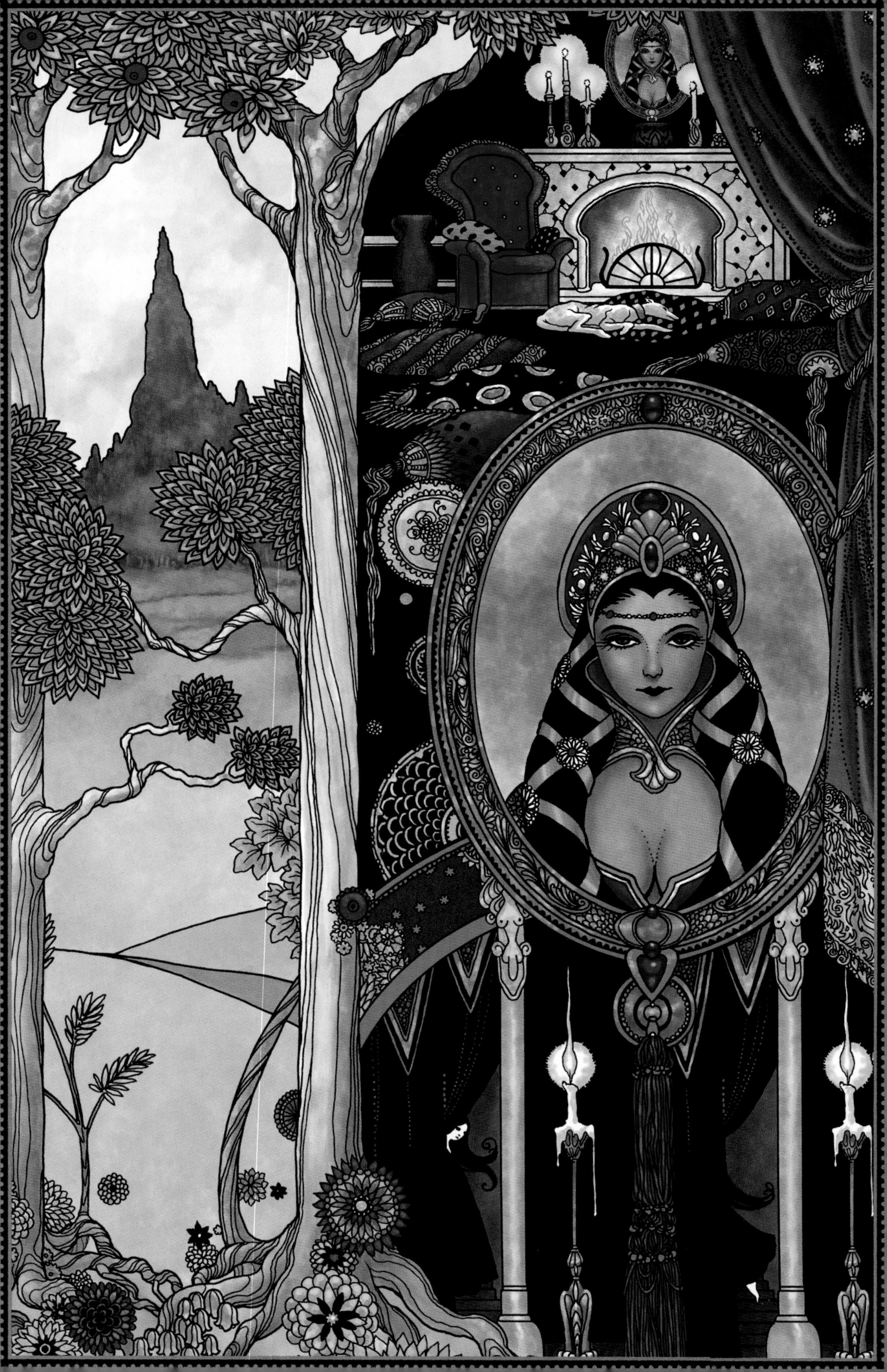

SNOW, GLASS, APPLES™

Story & Words
NEIL GAIMAN

Adaptation & Art
COLLEEN DORAN

Lettering
TODD KLEIN

DARK HORSE BOOKS

President and Publisher
MIKE RICHARDSON

Editor
DANIEL CHABON

Assistant Editor
CHUCK HOWITT

Designer
CINDY CACEREZ-SPRAGUE

Digital Art Technician
ANN GRAY

With respect and gratitude, the artist wishes to acknowledge her debt to
HARRY CLARKE
(Irish artist)
1889–1931

With color flatting assistance from
VAL TRULLINGER

Published by Dark Horse Books
A division of Dark Horse Comics LLC
10956 SE Main Street, Milwaukie, OR 97222

DarkHorse.com

To find a comic shop in your area, check out the Comic Shop Locator Service: comicshoplocator.com

First edition: August 2019
ISBN 978-1-50670-979-6

3 5 7 9 10 8 6 4 2
Printed in the United States of America

Library of Congress Cataloging-in-Publication Data

Names: Gaiman, Neil, author. | Doran, Colleen, 1963- artist.
Title: Snow, glass, apples / Neil Gaiman, stories and words ; Colleen Doran,
   adaptation and art.
Description: First edition. | Milwaukie, OR : Dark Horse Books, 2019.
Identifiers: LCCN 2019006854 | ISBN 9781506709796 (hardback)
Subjects: LCSH: Graphic novels. | BISAC: COMICS & GRAPHIC NOVELS / Fantasy. |
   COMICS & GRAPHIC NOVELS / Literary.
Classification: LCC PN6737.G3 S66 2019 | DDC 741.5/942--dc23
LC record available at https://lccn.loc.gov/2019006854

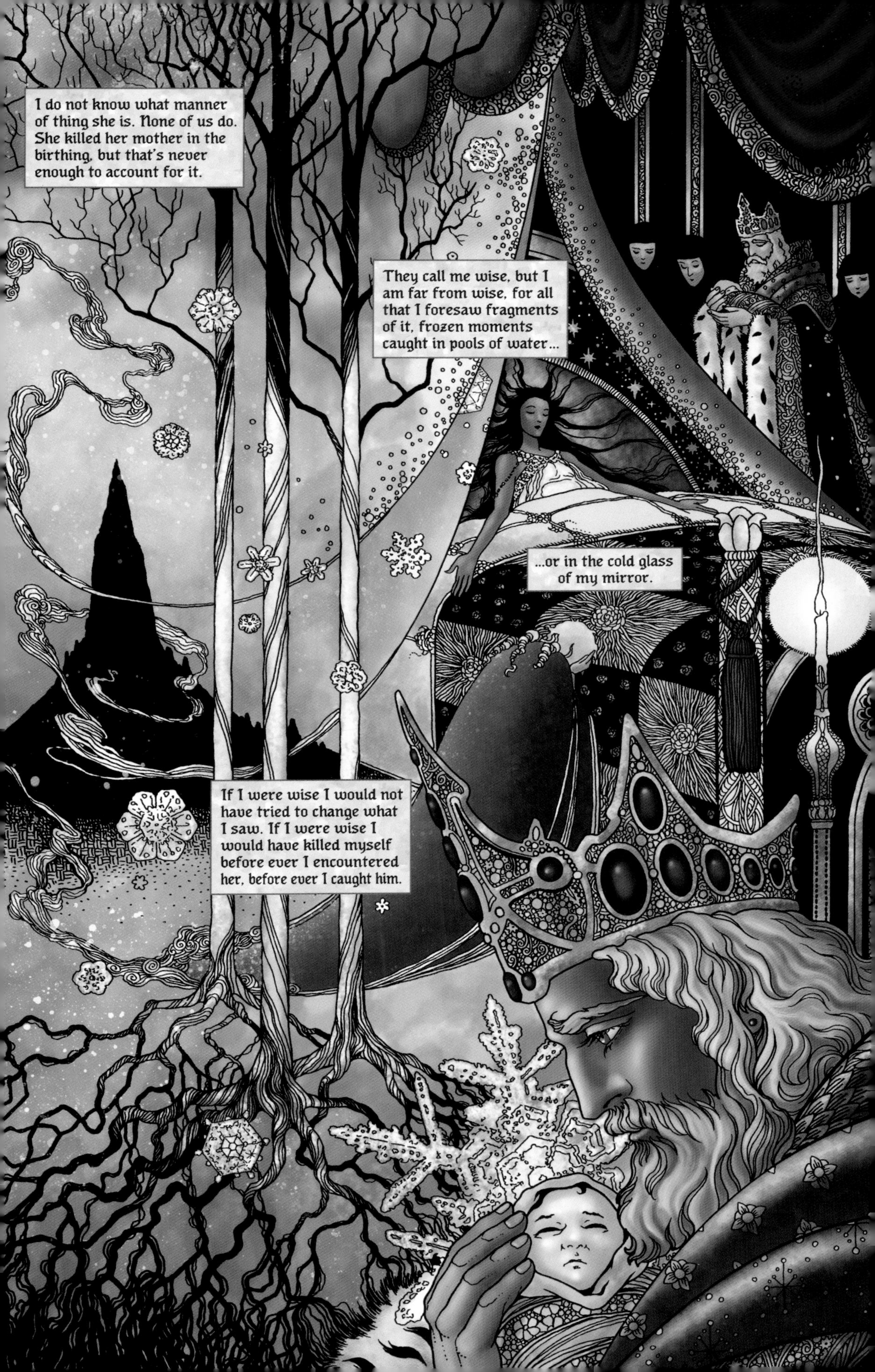
I do not know what manner of thing she is. None of us do. She killed her mother in the birthing, but that's never enough to account for it.
They call me wise, but I am far from wise, for all that I foresaw fragments of it, frozen moments caught in pools of water...
...or in the cold glass of my mirror.
If I were wise I would not have tried to change what I saw. If I were wise I would have killed myself before ever I encountered her, before ever I caught him.

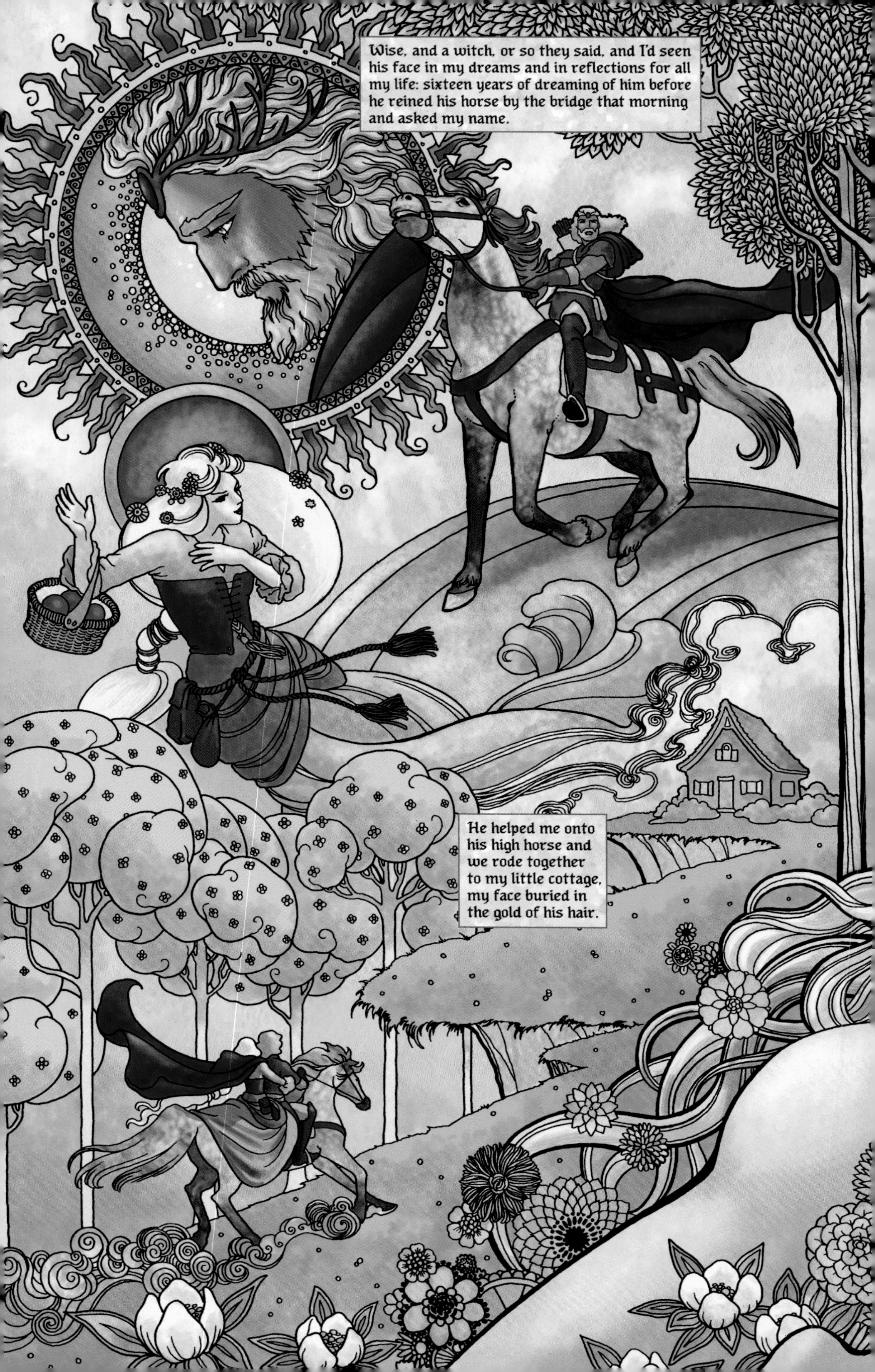
Wise, and a witch, or so they said, and I'd seen his face in my dreams and in reflections for all my life: sixteen years of dreaming of him before he reined his horse by the bridge that morning and asked my name.
He helped me onto his high horse and we rode together to my little cottage, my face buried in the gold of his hair.

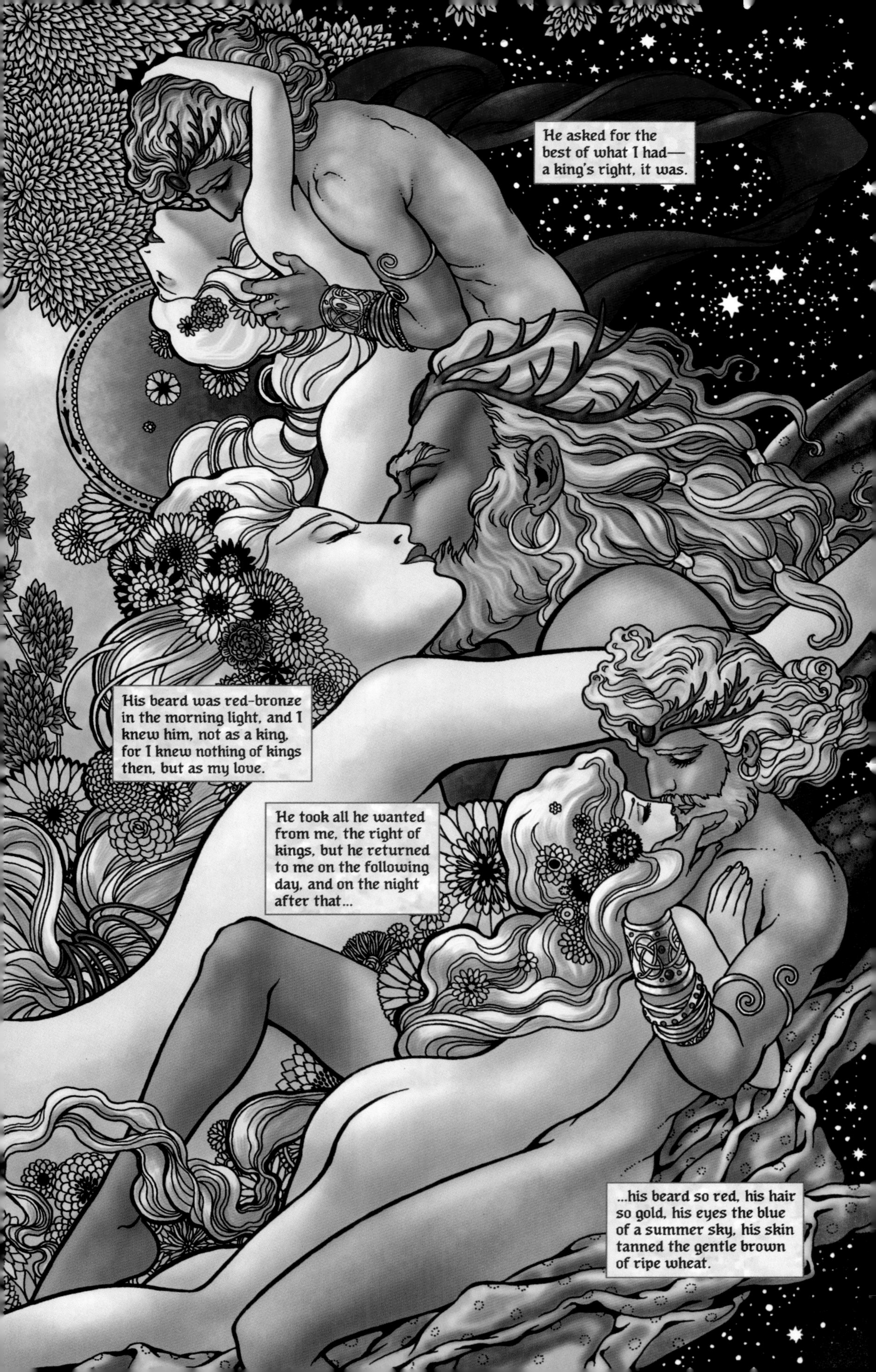
He asked for the best of what I had— a king's right, it was.
His beard was red-bronze in the morning light, and I knew him, not as a king, for I knew nothing of kings then, but as my love.
He took all he wanted from me, the right of kings, but he returned to me on the following day, and on the night after that...
...his beard so red, his hair so gold, his eyes the blue of a summer sky, his skin tanned the gentle brown of ripe wheat.

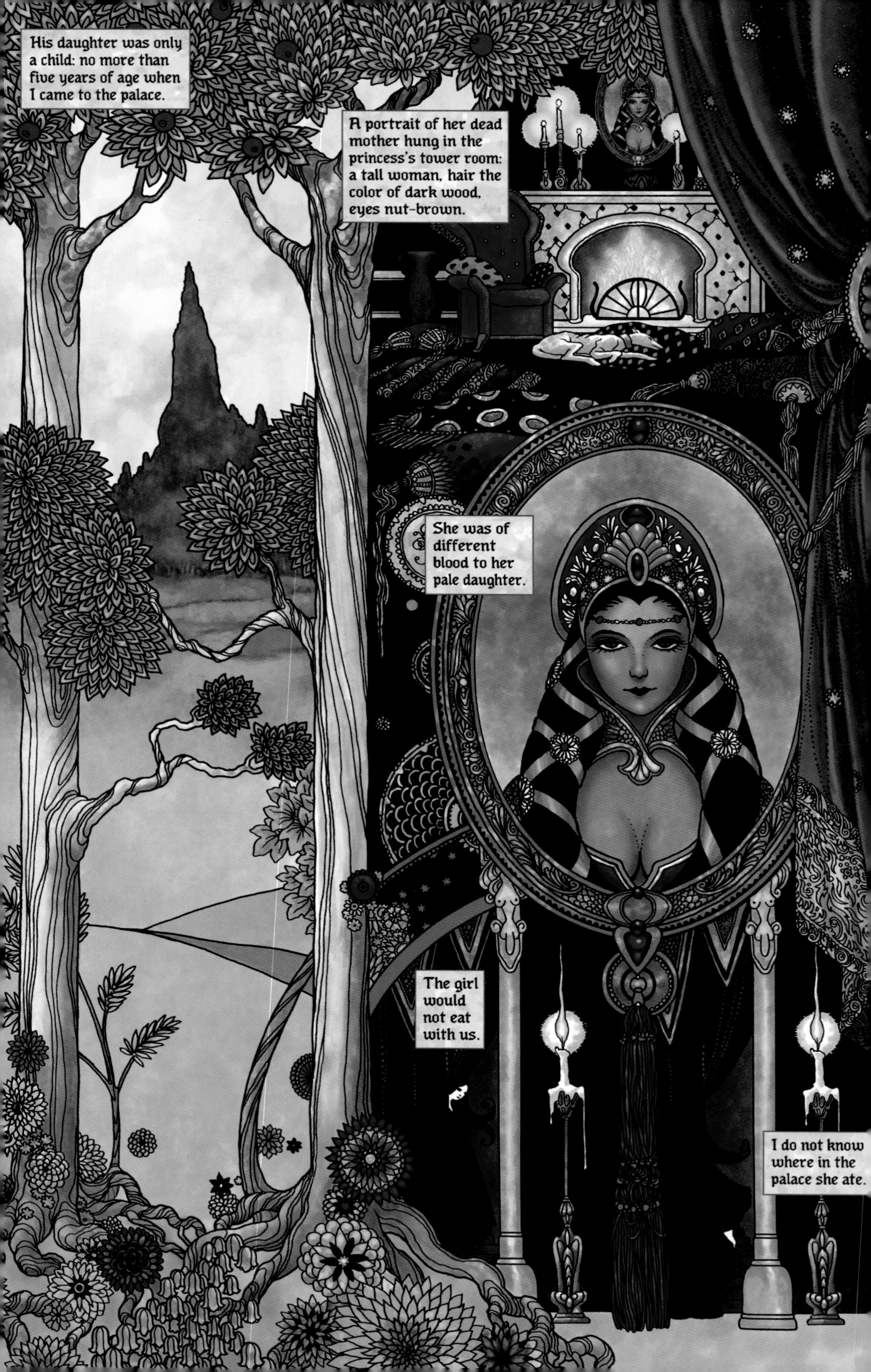
His daughter was only a child: no more than five years of age when I came to the palace.
A portrait of her dead mother hung in the princess's tower room: a tall woman, hair the color of dark wood, eyes nut-brown.
She was of different blood to her pale daughter.
The girl would not eat with us.
I do not know where in the palace she ate.

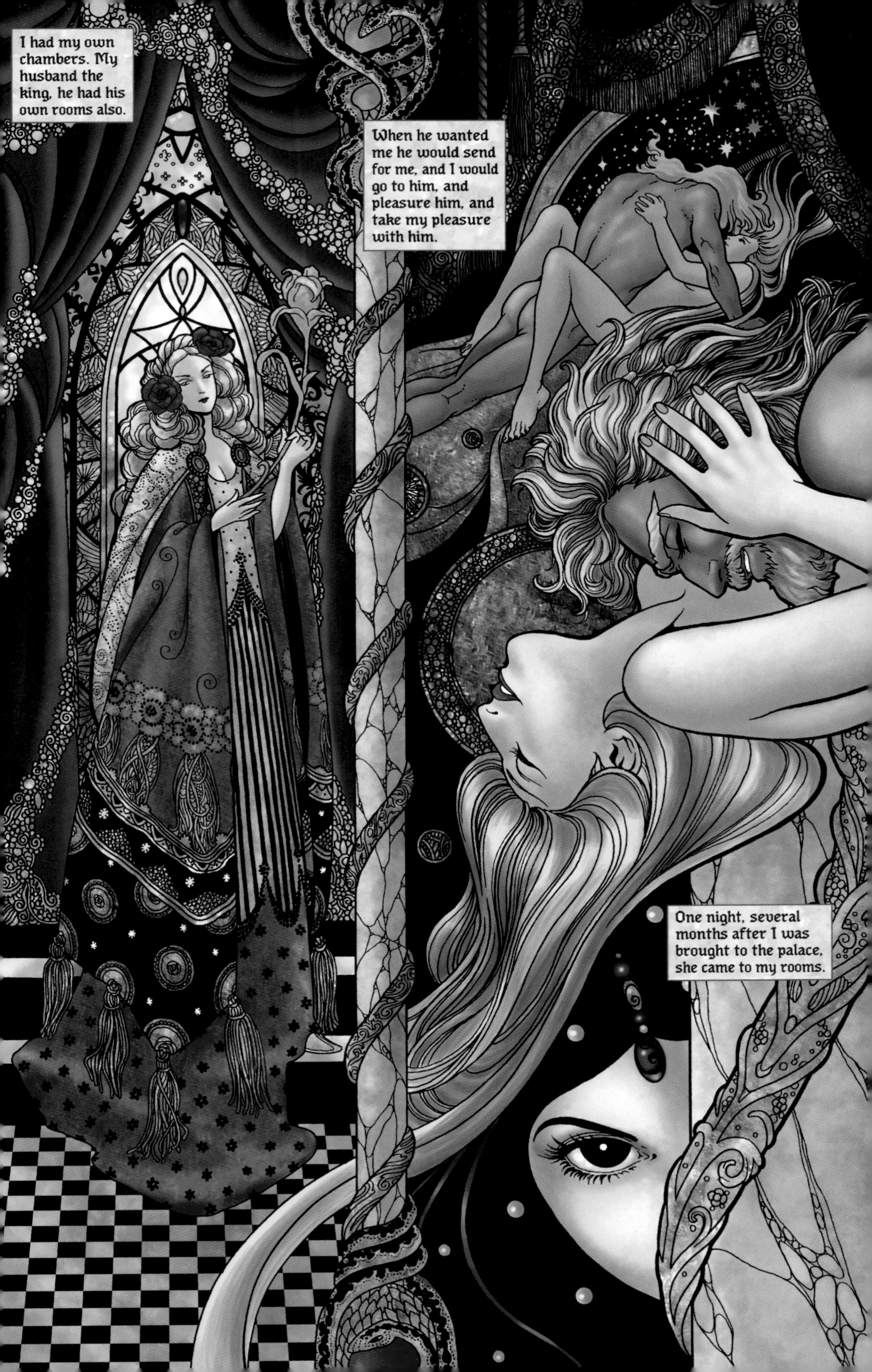
I had my own chambers. My husband the king, he had his own rooms also.
When he wanted me he would send for me, and I would go to him, and pleasure him, and take my pleasure with him.
One night, several months after I was brought to the palace, she came to my rooms.

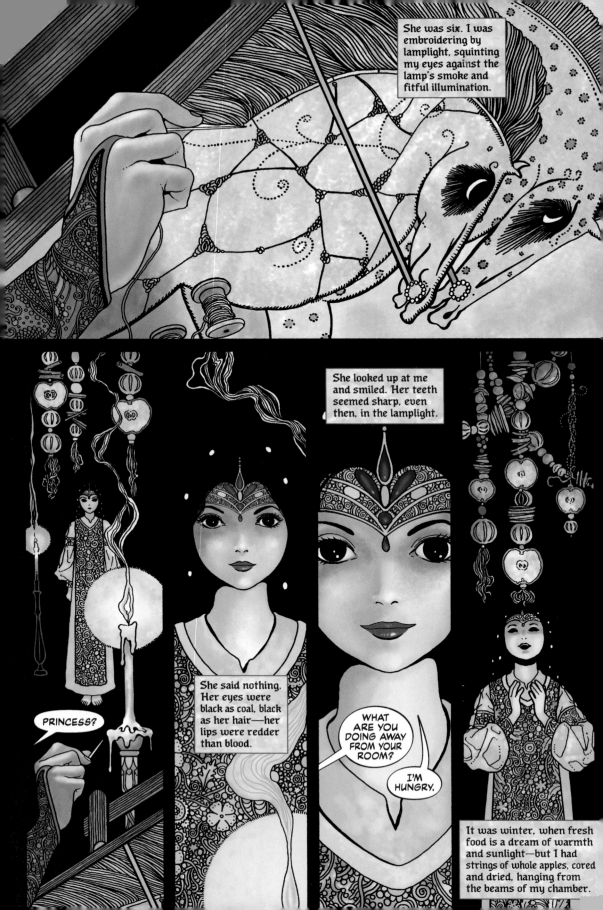

She was six. I was embroidering by lamplight, squinting my eyes against the lamp's smoke and fitful illumination.

She looked up at me and smiled. Her teeth seemed sharp, even then, in the lamplight.

PRINCESS?

She said nothing. Her eyes were black as coal, black as her hair—her lips were redder than blood.

WHAT ARE YOU DOING AWAY FROM YOUR ROOM?

I'M HUNGRY.

It was winter, when fresh food is a dream of warmth and sunlight—but I had strings of whole apples, cored and dried, hanging from the beams of my chamber.

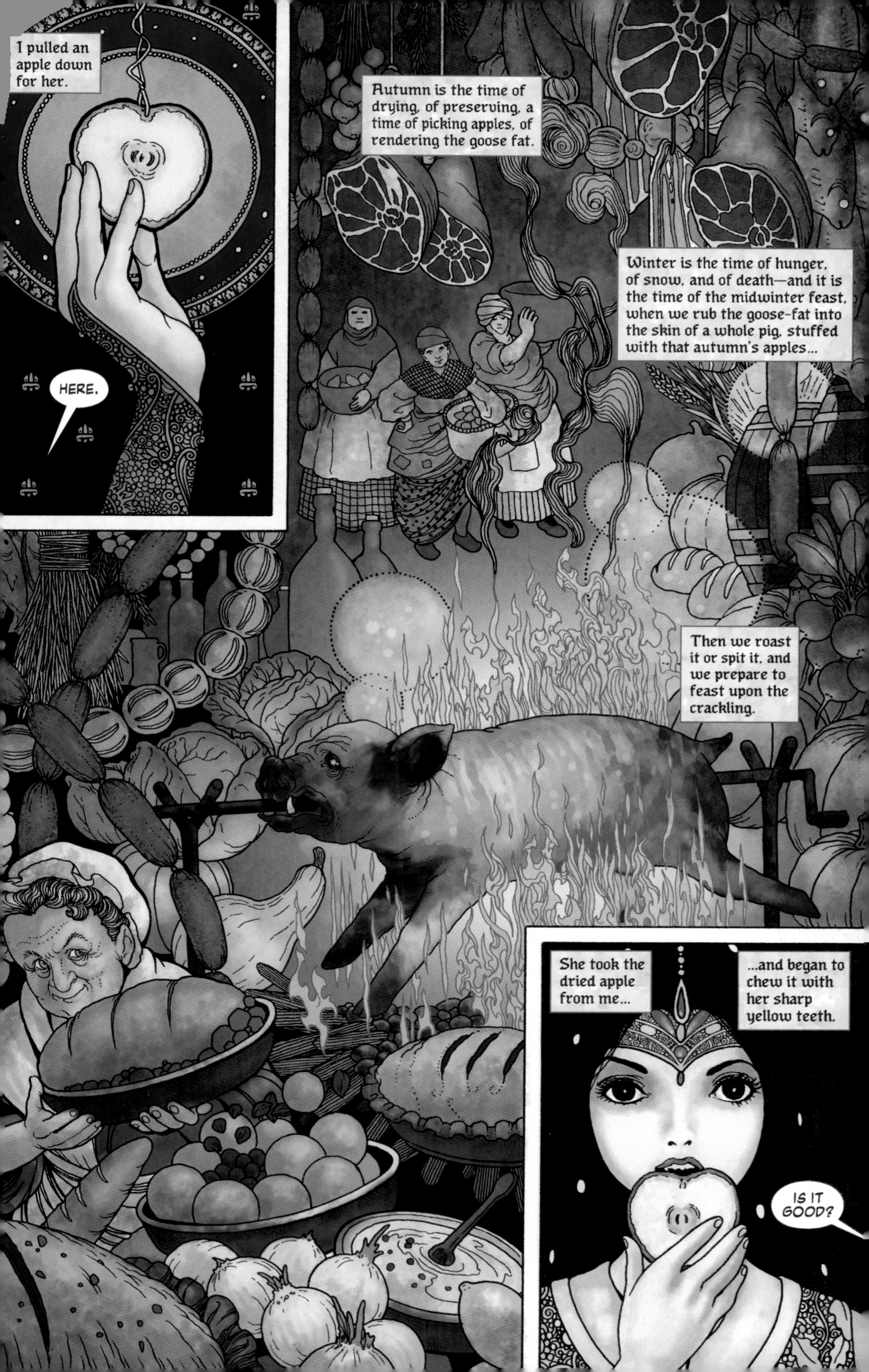
I pulled an apple down for her.
HERE.
Autumn is the time of drying, of preserving, a time of picking apples, of rendering the goose fat.
Winter is the time of hunger, of snow, and of death—and it is the time of the midwinter feast, when we rub the goose-fat into the skin of a whole pig, stuffed with that autumn's apples...
Then we roast it or spit it, and we prepare to feast upon the crackling.
She took the dried apple from me...
...and began to chew it with her sharp yellow teeth.
IS IT GOOD?

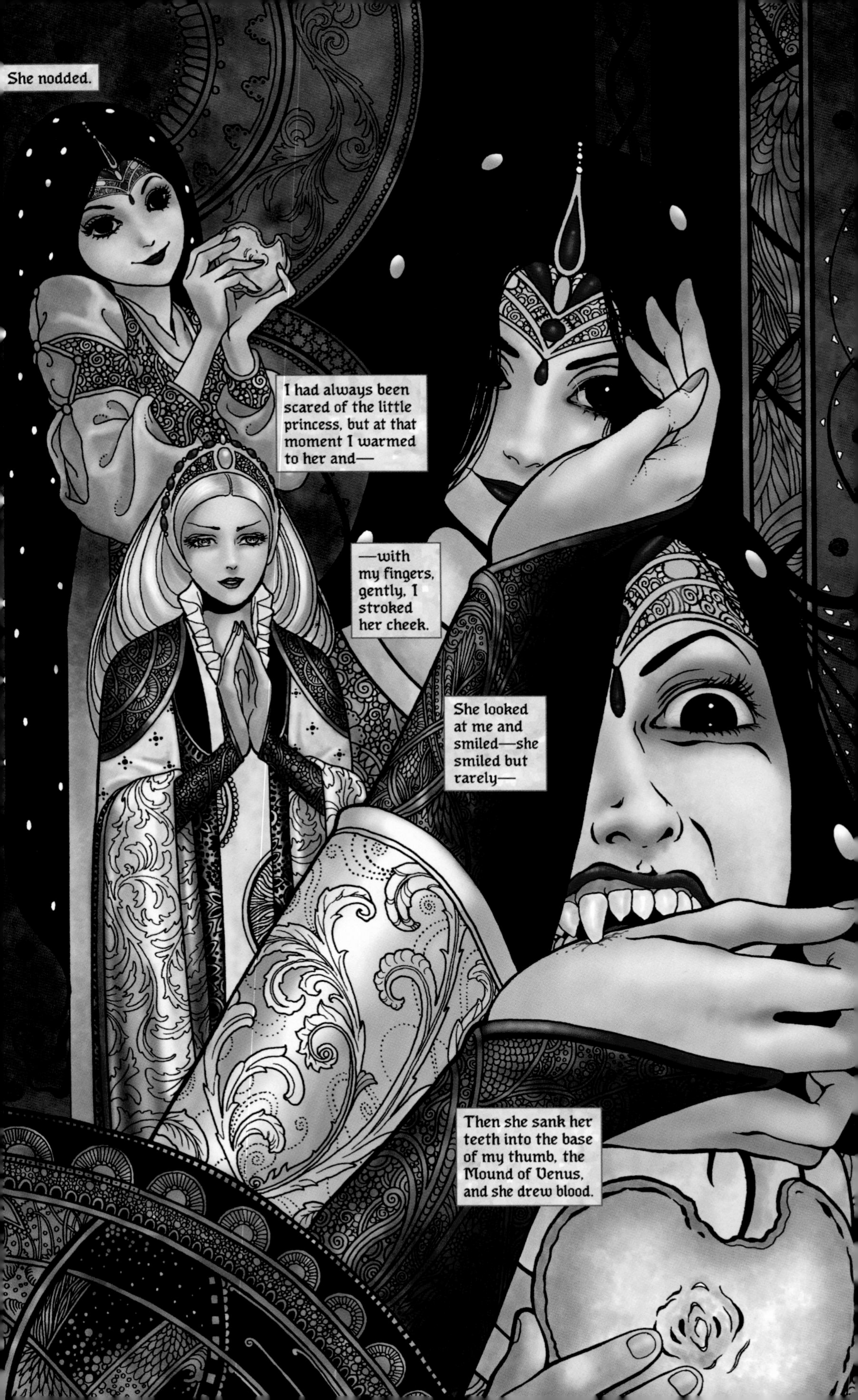
She nodded.
I had always been scared of the little princess, but at that moment I warmed to her and—
—with my fingers, gently, I stroked her cheek.
She looked at me and smiled—she smiled but rarely—
Then she sank her teeth into the base of my thumb, the Mound of Venus, and she drew blood.

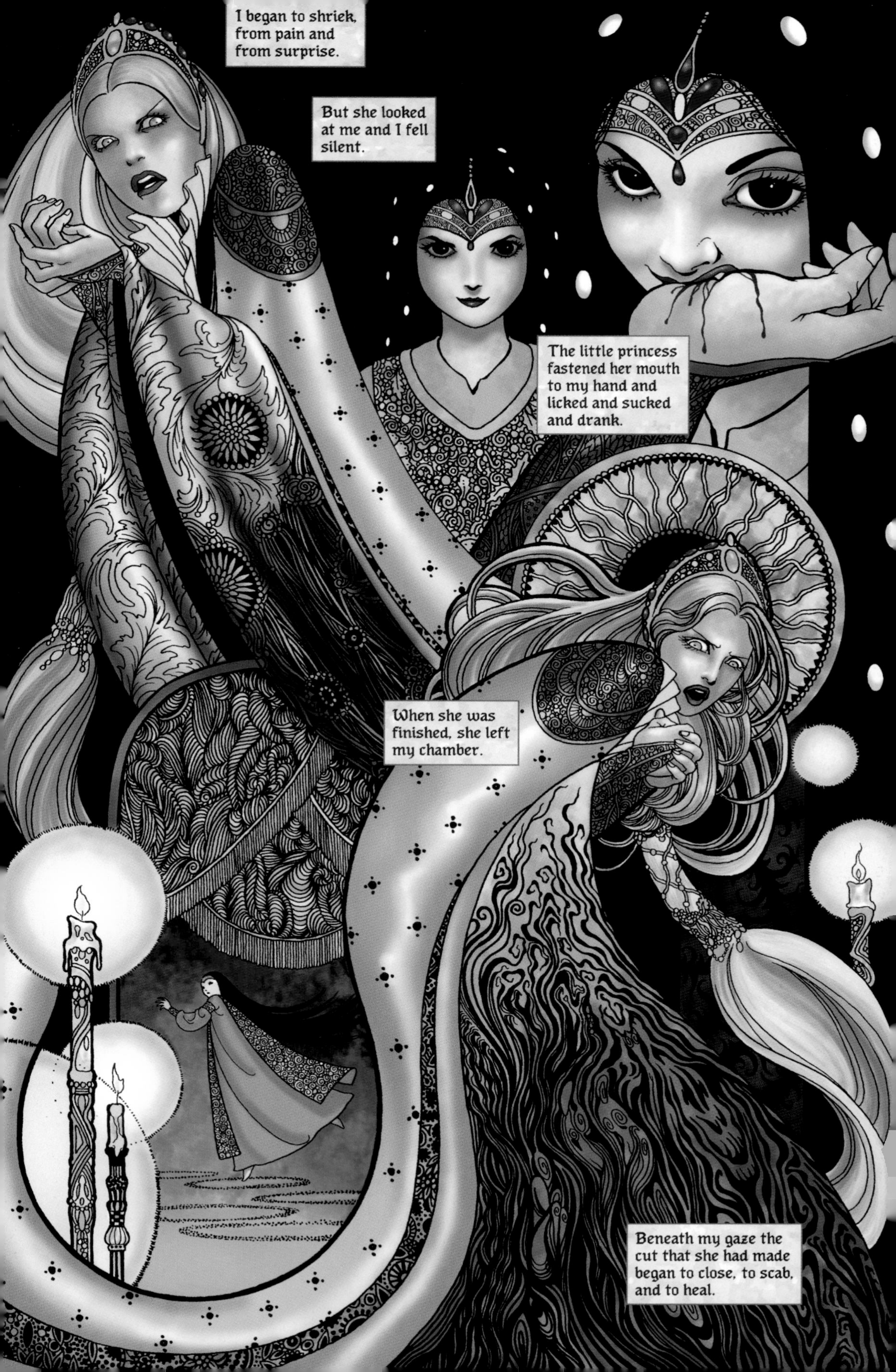
I began to shriek, from pain and from surprise.
But she looked at me and I fell silent.
The little princess fastened her mouth to my hand and licked and sucked and drank.
When she was finished, she left my chamber.
Beneath my gaze the cut that she had made began to close, to scab, and to heal.

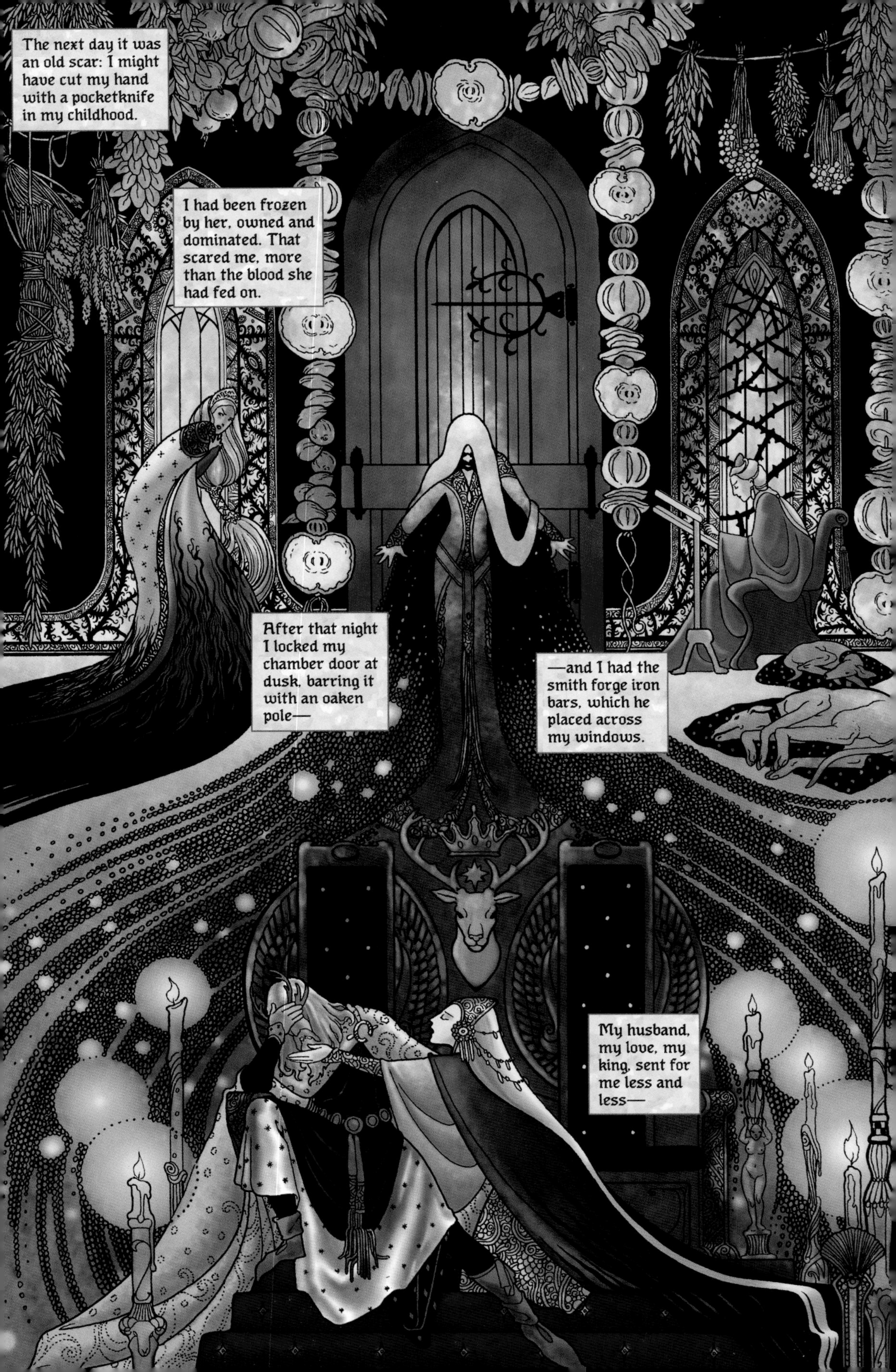
The next day it was an old scar: I might have cut my hand with a pocketknife in my childhood.
I had been frozen by her, owned and dominated. That scared me, more than the blood she had fed on.
After that night I locked my chamber door at dusk, barring it with an oaken pole—
—and I had the smith forge iron bars, which he placed across my windows.
My husband, my love, my king, sent for me less and less—

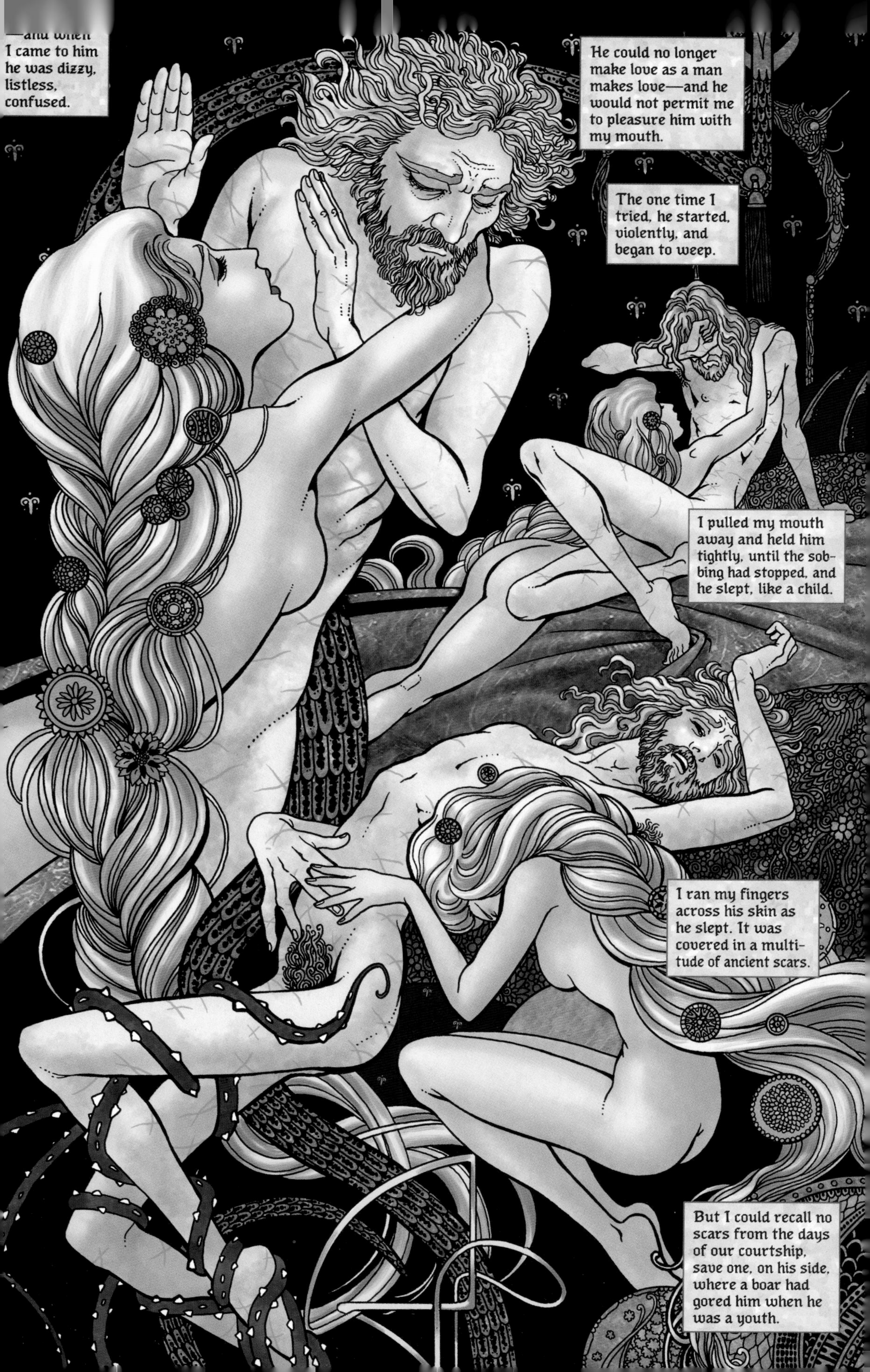
I came to him he was dizzy, listless, confused.
He could no longer make love as a man makes love—and he would not permit me to pleasure him with my mouth.
The one time I tried, he started, violently, and began to weep.
I pulled my mouth away and held him tightly, until the sobbing had stopped, and he slept, like a child.
I ran my fingers across his skin as he slept. It was covered in a multitude of ancient scars.
But I could recall no scars from the days of our courtship, save one, on his side, where a boar had gored him when he was a youth.

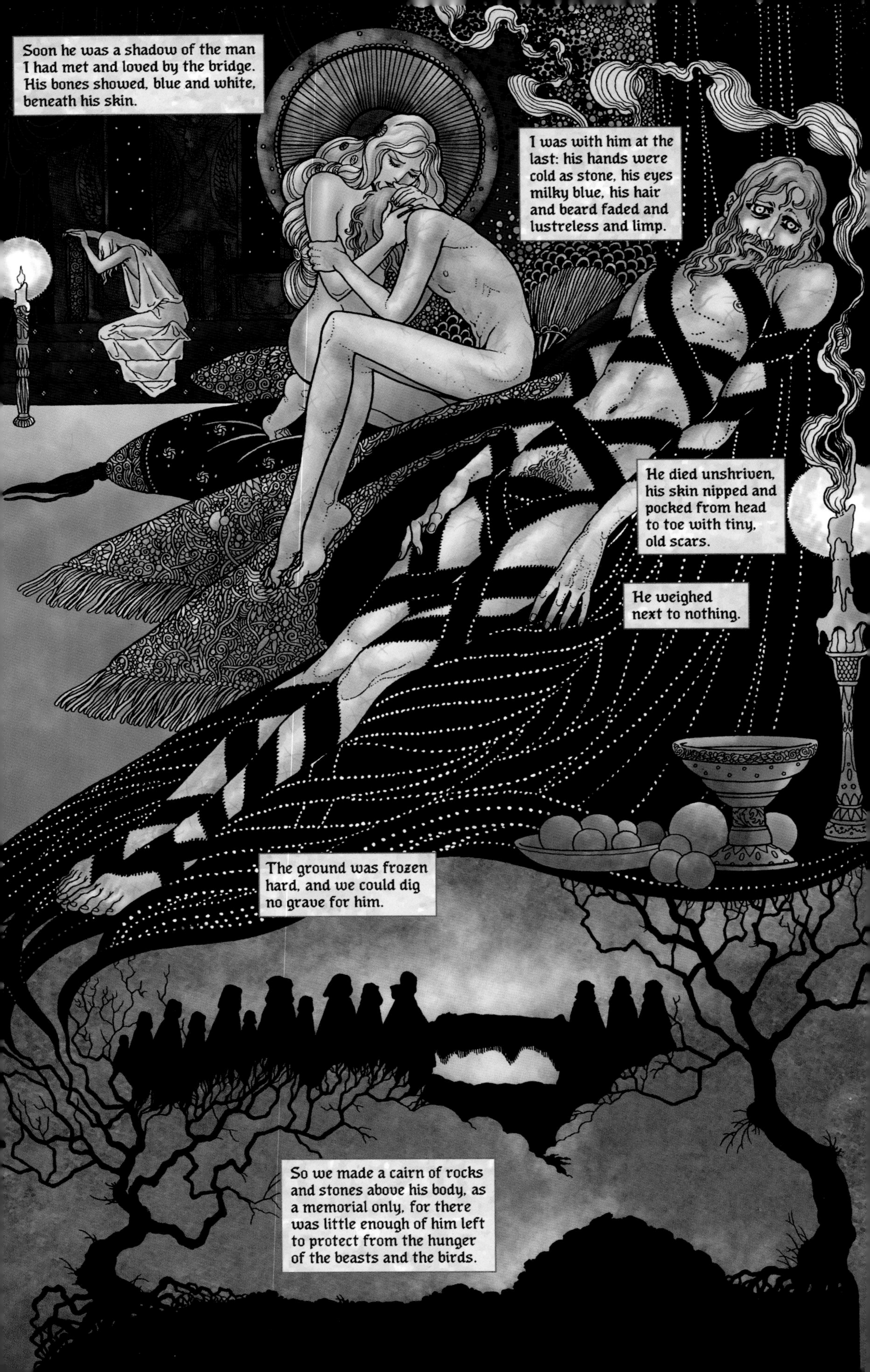

Soon he was a shadow of the man I had met and loved by the bridge. His bones showed, blue and white, beneath his skin.
I was with him at the last: his hands were cold as stone, his eyes milky blue, his hair and beard faded and lustreless and limp.
He died unshriven, his skin nipped and pocked from head to toe with tiny, old scars.
He weighed next to nothing.
The ground was frozen hard, and we could dig no grave for him.
So we made a cairn of rocks and stones above his body, as a memorial only, for there was little enough of him left to protect from the hunger of the beasts and the birds.

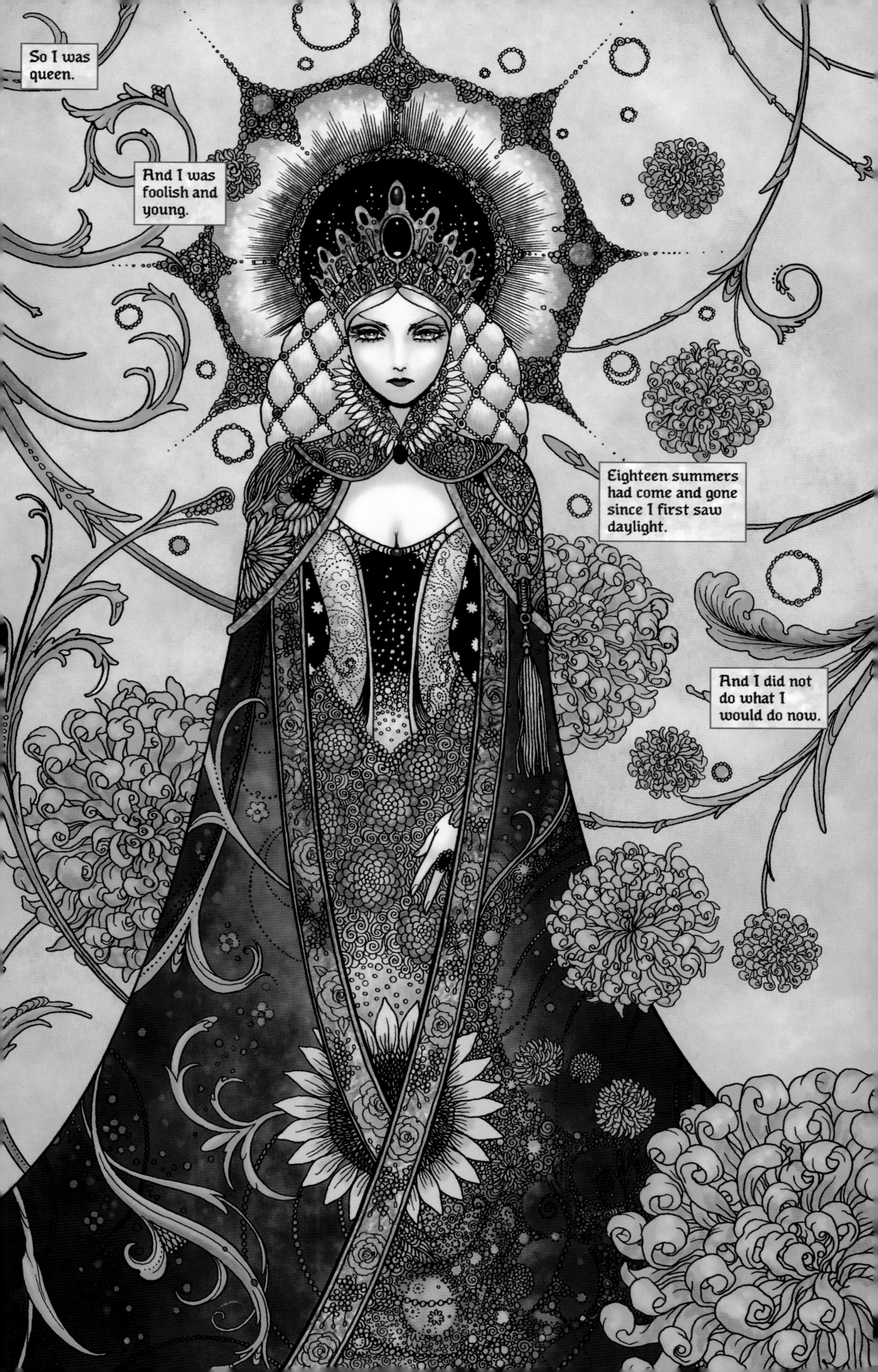
So I was queen.
And I was foolish and young.
Eighteen summers had come and gone since I first saw daylight.
And I did not do what I would do now.

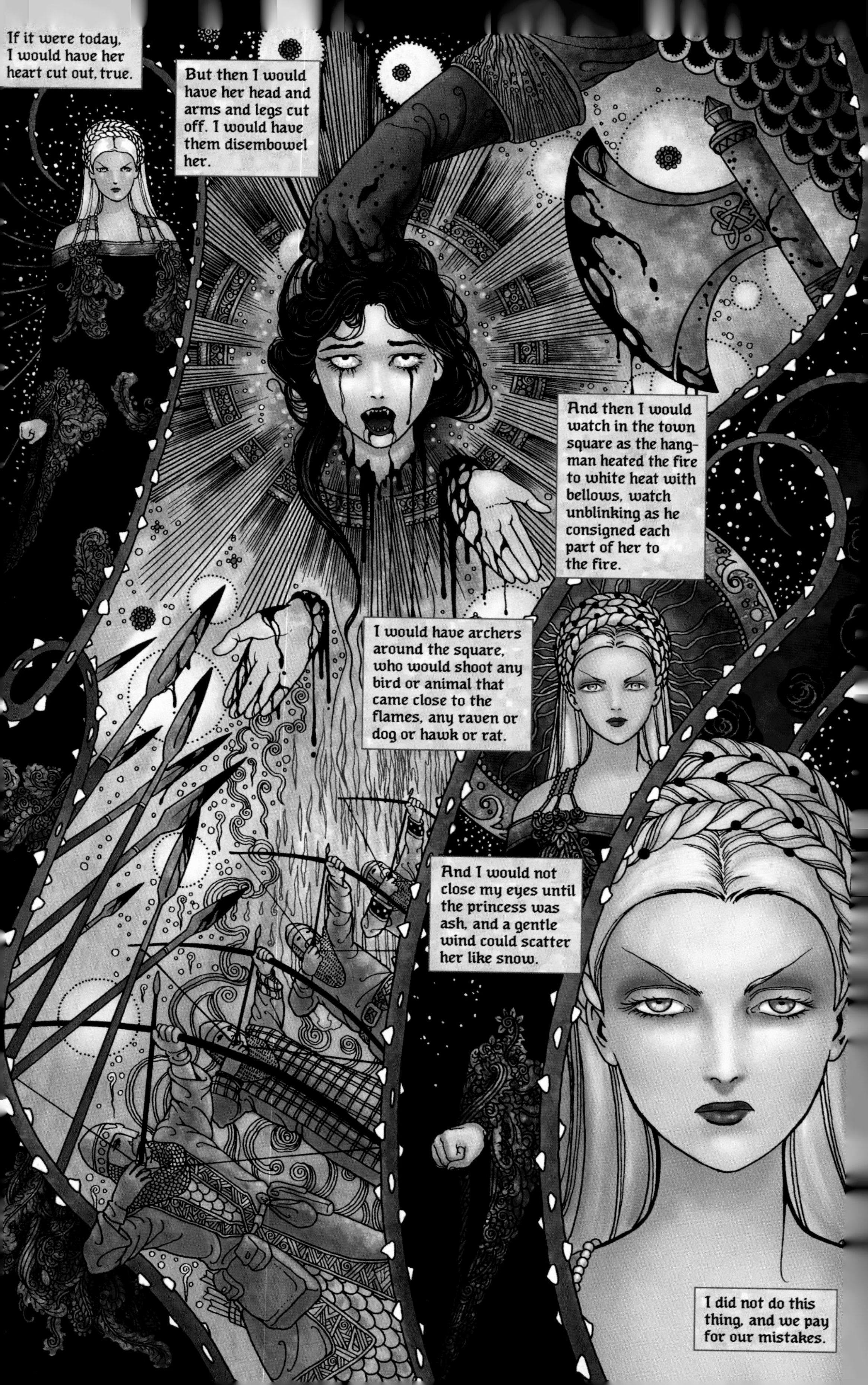
If it were today, I would have her heart cut out, true.
But then I would have her head and arms and legs cut off. I would have them disembowel her.
And then I would watch in the town square as the hang-man heated the fire to white heat with bellows, watch unblinking as he consigned each part of her to the fire.
I would have archers around the square, who would shoot any bird or animal that came close to the flames, any raven or dog or hawk or rat.
And I would not close my eyes until the princess was ash, and a gentle wind could scatter her like snow.
I did not do this thing, and we pay for our mistakes.

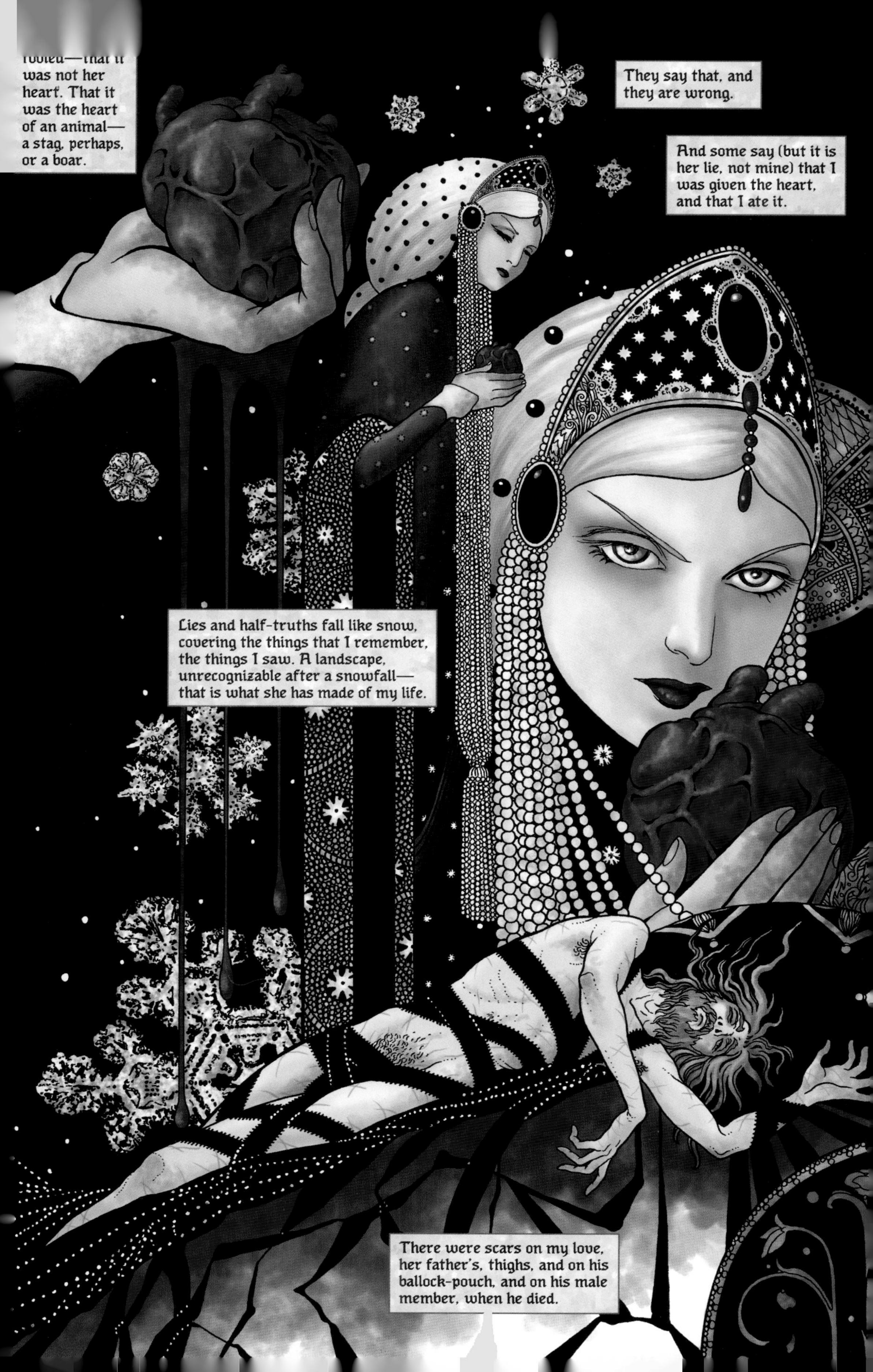
fooled—that it was not her heart. That it was the heart of an animal—a stag, perhaps, or a boar.
They say that, and they are wrong.
And some say (but it is her lie, not mine) that I was given the heart, and that I ate it.
Lies and half-truths fall like snow, covering the things that I remember, the things I saw. A landscape, unrecognizable after a snowfall—that is what she has made of my life.
There were scars on my love, her father's, thighs, and on his ballock-pouch, and on his male member, when he died.

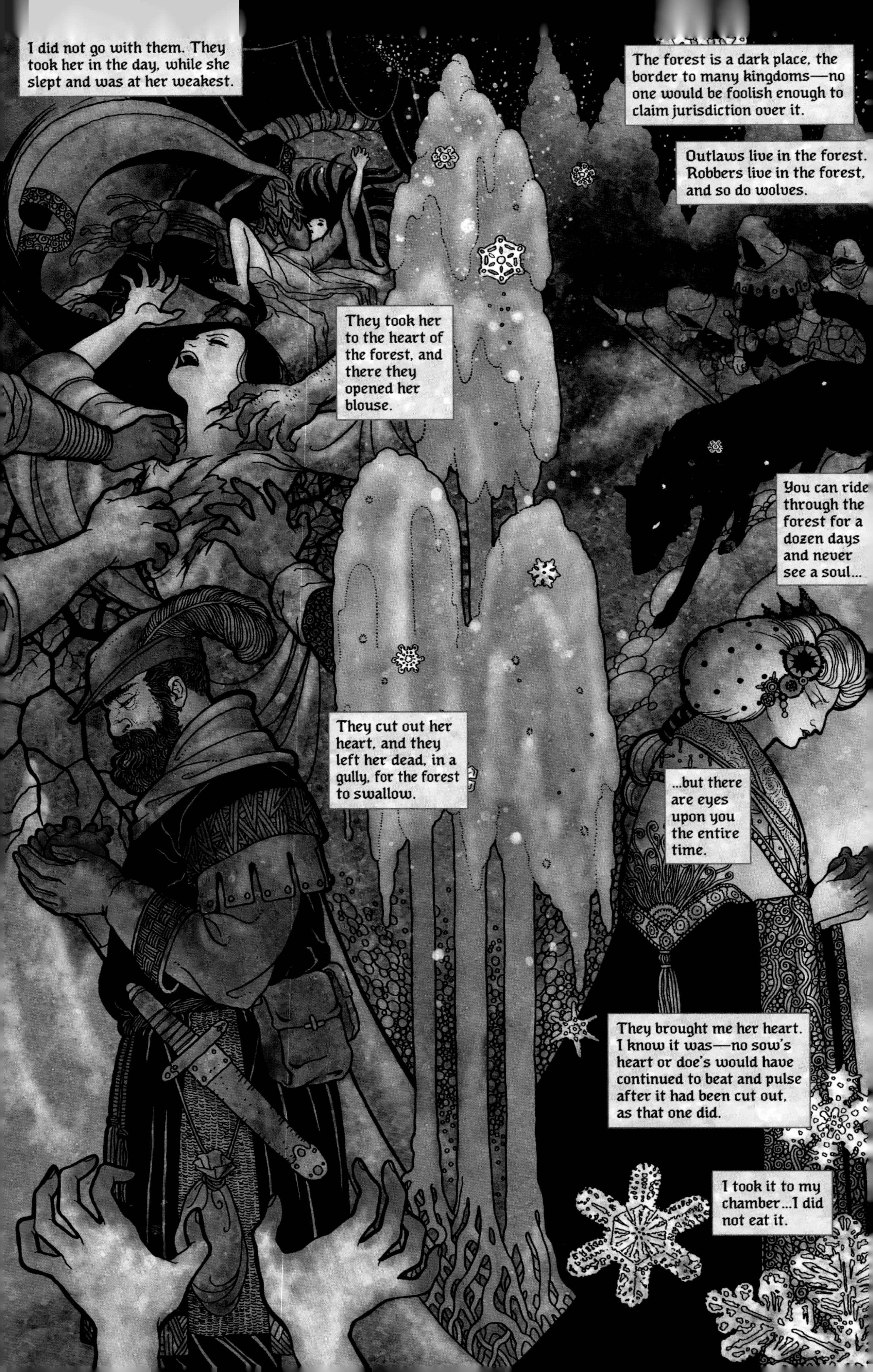
I did not go with them. They took her in the day, while she slept and was at her weakest.
The forest is a dark place, the border to many kingdoms—no one would be foolish enough to claim jurisdiction over it.
Outlaws live in the forest. Robbers live in the forest, and so do wolves.
They took her to the heart of the forest, and there they opened her blouse.
You can ride through the forest for a dozen days and never see a soul...
They cut out her heart, and they left her dead, in a gully, for the forest to swallow.
...but there are eyes upon you the entire time.
They brought me her heart. I know it was—no sow's heart or doe's would have continued to beat and pulse after it had been cut out, as that one did.
I took it to my chamber...I did not eat it.

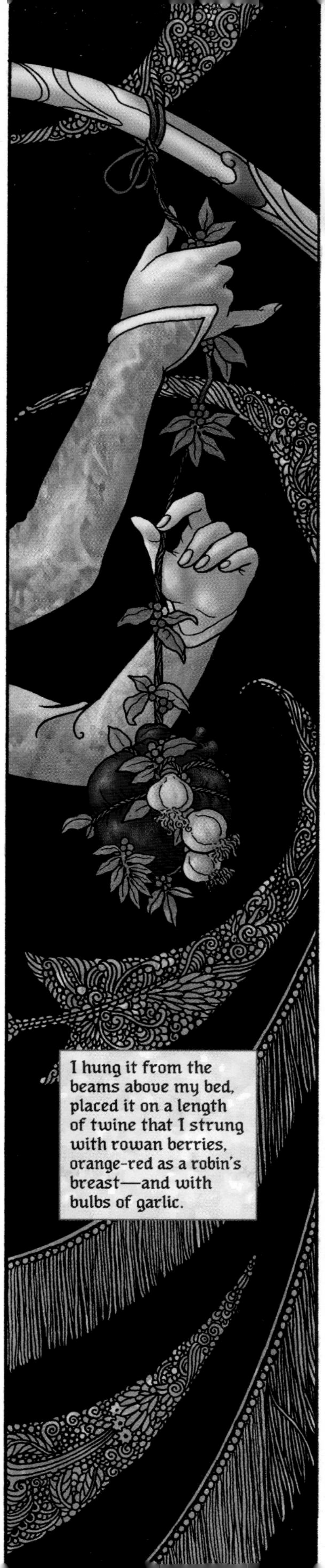
I hung it from the beams above my bed, placed it on a length of twine that I strung with rowan berries, orange-red as a robin's breast—and with bulbs of garlic.

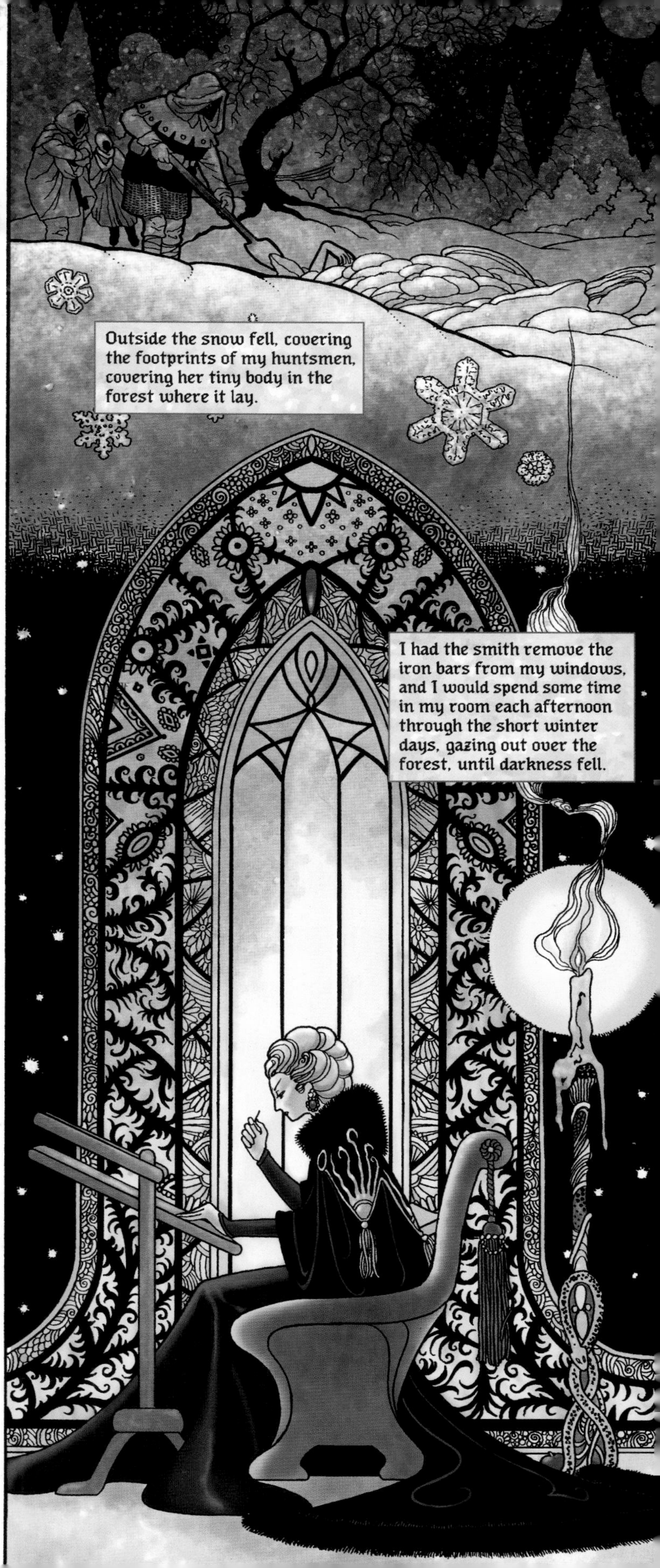
Outside the snow fell, covering the footprints of my huntsmen, covering her tiny body in the forest where it lay.
I had the smith remove the iron bars from my windows, and I would spend some time in my room each afternoon through the short winter days, gazing out over the forest, until darkness fell.

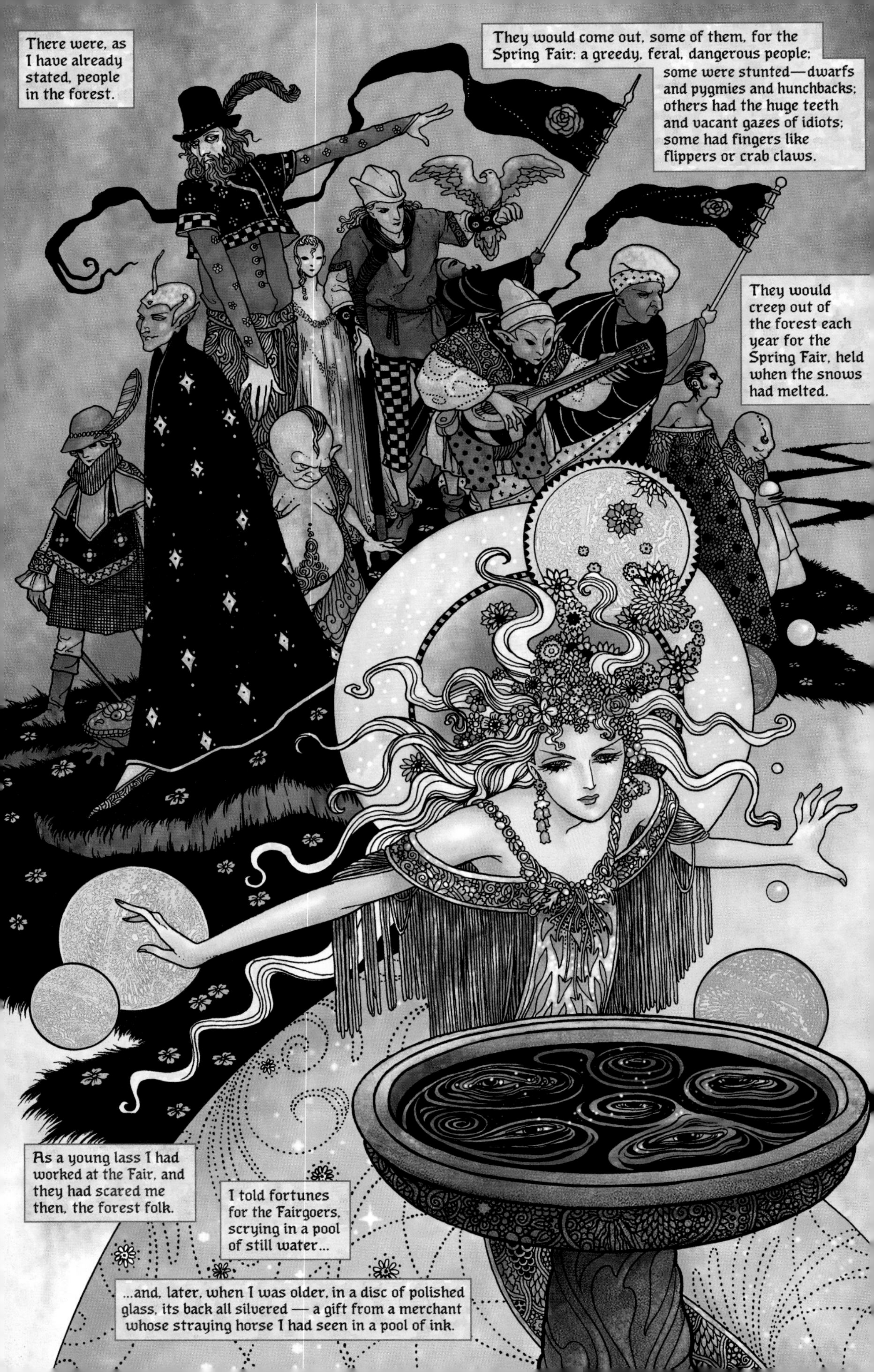
There were, as I have already stated, people in the forest.
They would come out, some of them, for the Spring Fair: a greedy, feral, dangerous people; some were stunted—dwarfs and pygmies and hunchbacks; others had the huge teeth and vacant gazes of idiots; some had fingers like flippers or crab claws.
They would creep out of the forest each year for the Spring Fair, held when the snows had melted.
As a young lass I had worked at the Fair, and they had scared me then, the forest folk.
I told fortunes for the Fairgoers, scrying in a pool of still water...
...and, later, when I was older, in a disc of polished glass, its back all silvered — a gift from a merchant whose straying horse I had seen in a pool of ink.

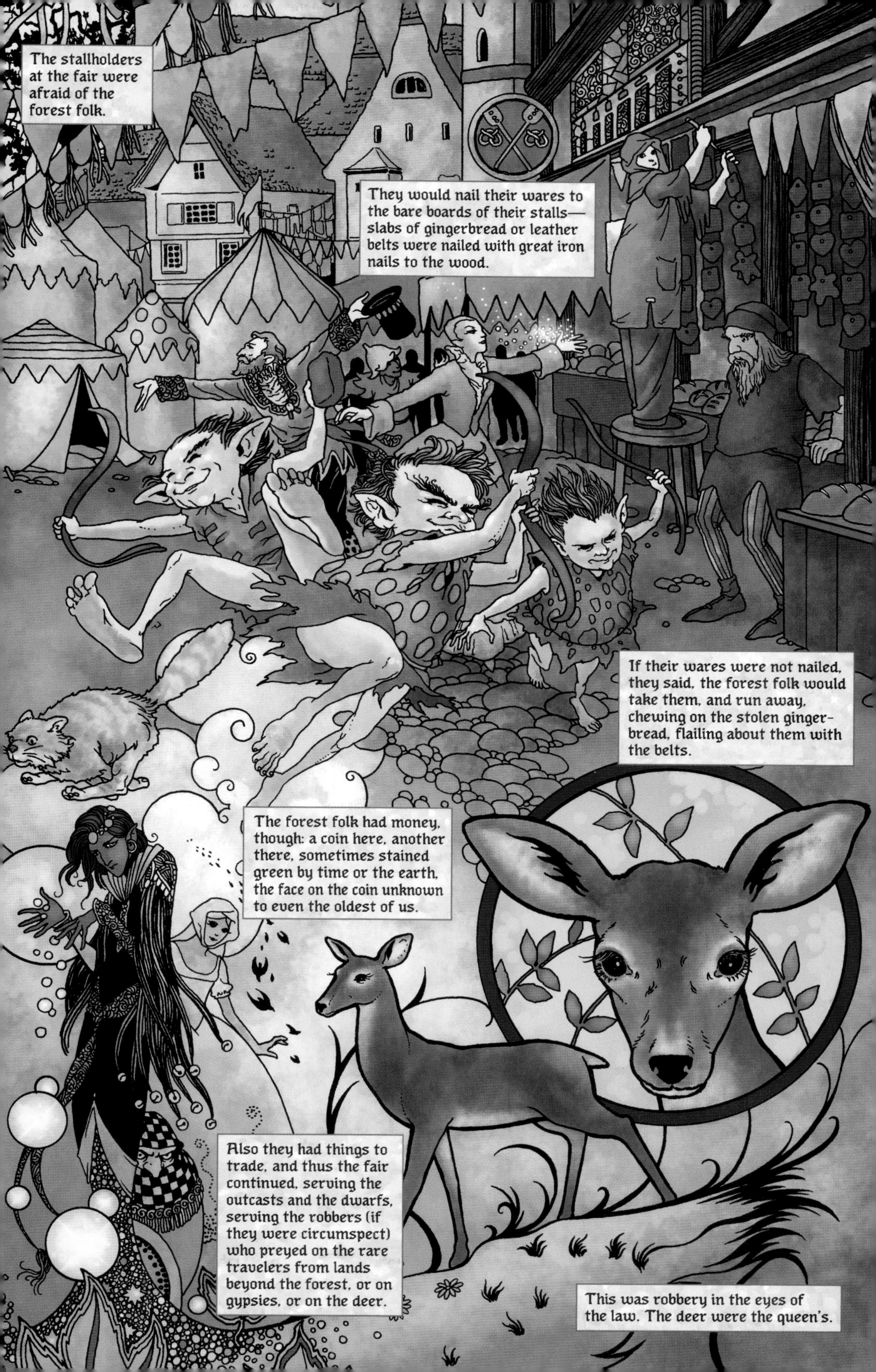
The stallholders at the fair were afraid of the forest folk.
They would nail their wares to the bare boards of their stalls—slabs of gingerbread or leather belts were nailed with great iron nails to the wood.
If their wares were not nailed, they said, the forest folk would take them, and run away, chewing on the stolen gingerbread, flailing about them with the belts.
The forest folk had money, though: a coin here, another there, sometimes stained green by time or the earth, the face on the coin unknown to even the oldest of us.
Also they had things to trade, and thus the fair continued, serving the outcasts and the dwarfs, serving the robbers (if they were circumspect) who preyed on the rare travelers from lands beyond the forest, or on gypsies, or on the deer.
This was robbery in the eyes of the law. The deer were the queen's.

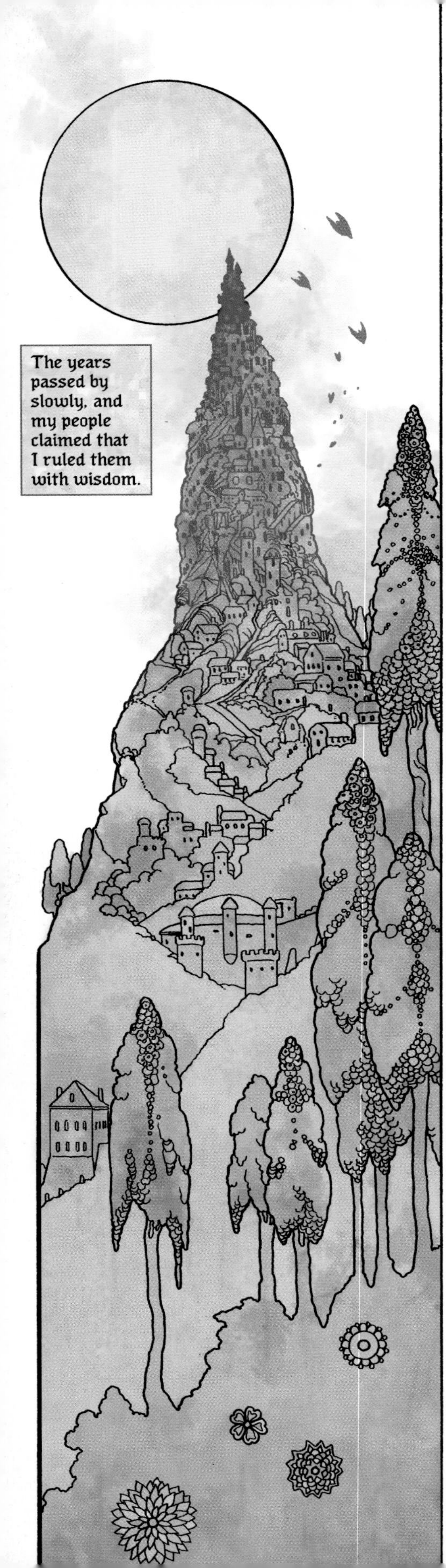
The years passed by slowly, and my people claimed that I ruled them with wisdom.

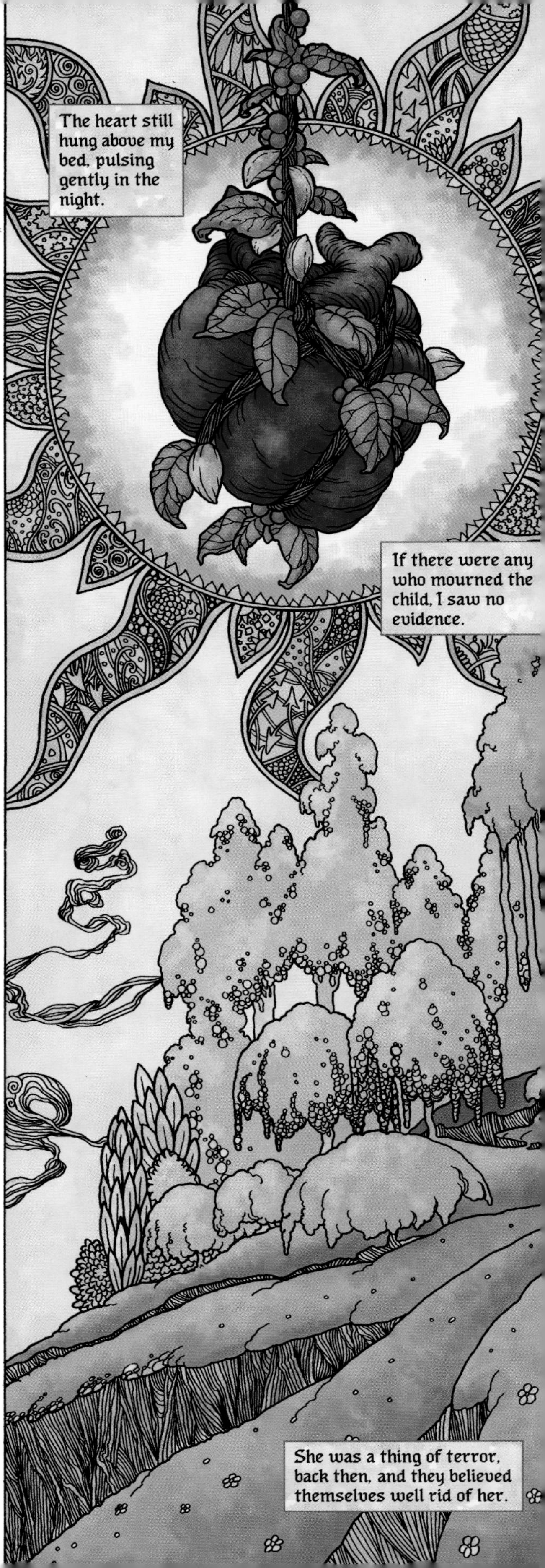
The heart still hung above my bed, pulsing gently in the night.
If there were any who mourned the child, I saw no evidence.
She was a thing of terror, back then, and they believed themselves well rid of her.

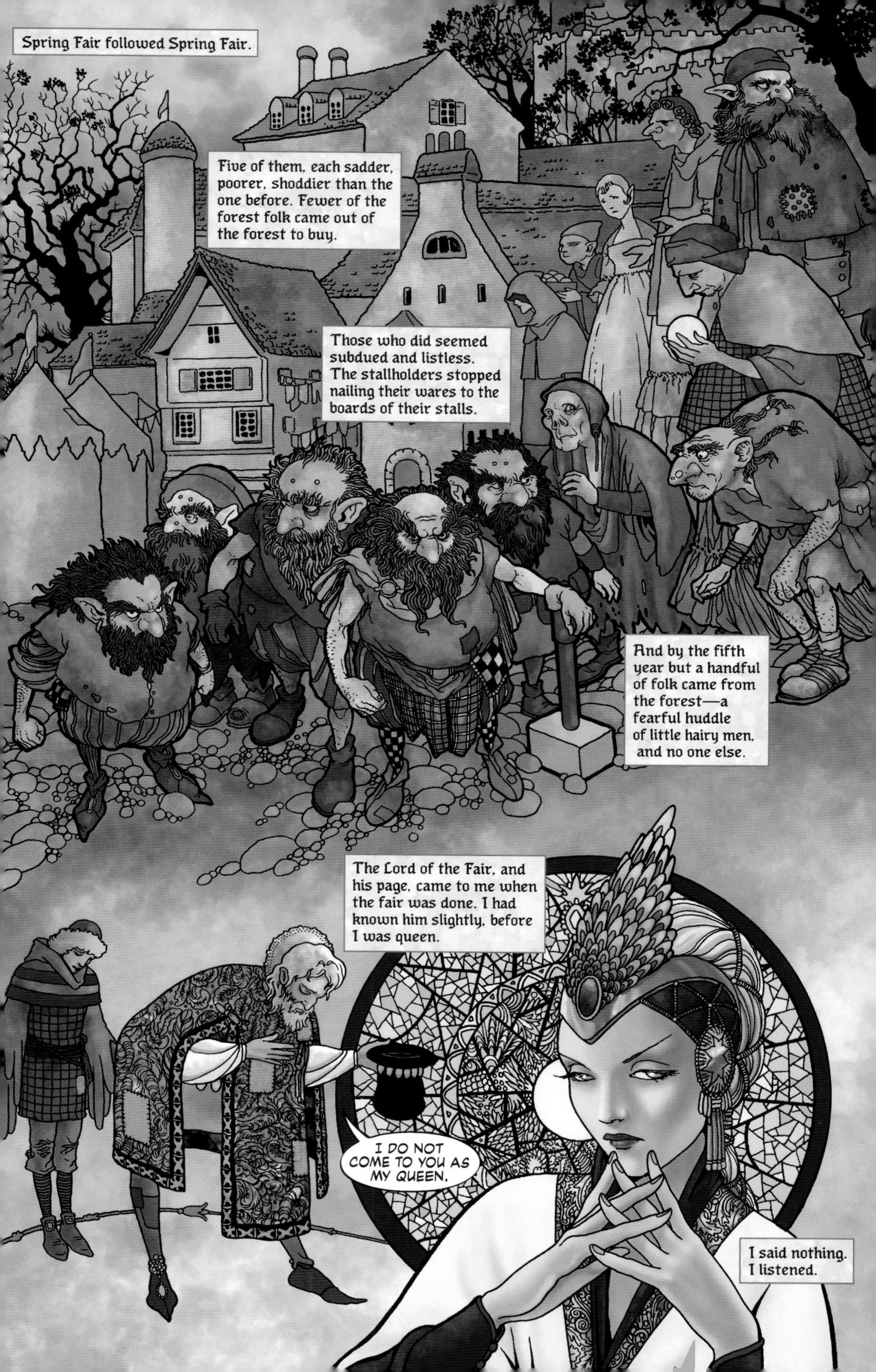
Spring Fair followed Spring Fair.
Five of them, each sadder, poorer, shoddier than the one before. Fewer of the forest folk came out of the forest to buy.
Those who did seemed subdued and listless. The stallholders stopped nailing their wares to the boards of their stalls.
And by the fifth year but a handful of folk came from the forest—a fearful huddle of little hairy men, and no one else.
The Lord of the Fair, and his page, came to me when the fair was done. I had known him slightly, before I was queen.
I DO NOT COME TO YOU AS MY QUEEN.
I said nothing. I listened.

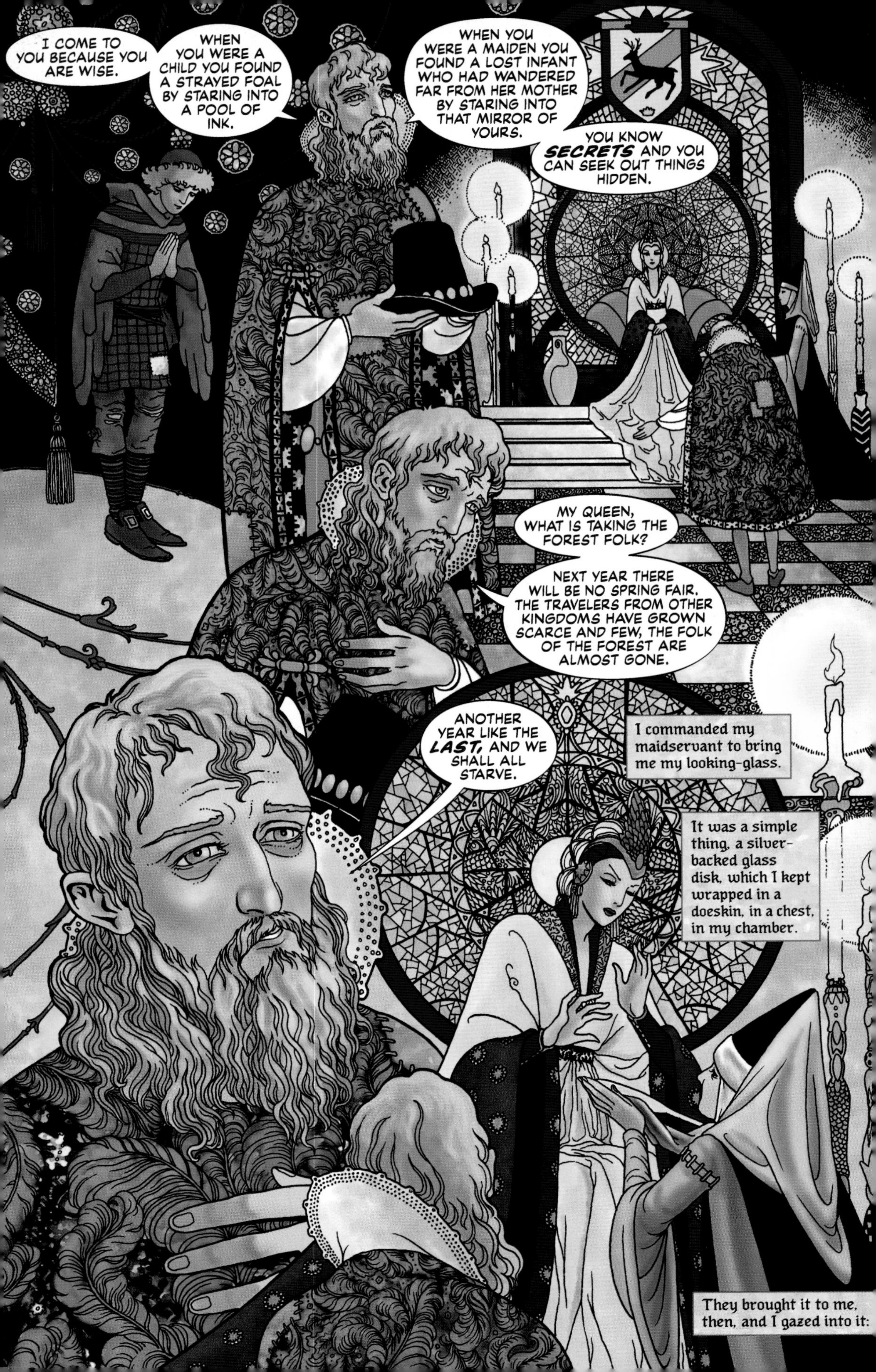
I COME TO YOU BECAUSE YOU ARE WISE.
WHEN YOU WERE A CHILD YOU FOUND A STRAYED FOAL BY STARING INTO A POOL OF INK.
WHEN YOU WERE A MAIDEN YOU FOUND A LOST INFANT WHO HAD WANDERED FAR FROM HER MOTHER BY STARING INTO THAT MIRROR OF YOURS.
YOU KNOW SECRETS AND YOU CAN SEEK OUT THINGS HIDDEN.
MY QUEEN, WHAT IS TAKING THE FOREST FOLK?
NEXT YEAR THERE WILL BE NO SPRING FAIR. THE TRAVELERS FROM OTHER KINGDOMS HAVE GROWN SCARCE AND FEW, THE FOLK OF THE FOREST ARE ALMOST GONE.
ANOTHER YEAR LIKE THE LAST, AND WE SHALL ALL STARVE.
I commanded my maidservant to bring me my looking-glass.
It was a simple thing, a silver-backed glass disk, which I kept wrapped in a doeskin, in a chest, in my chamber.
They brought it to me, then, and I gazed into it:

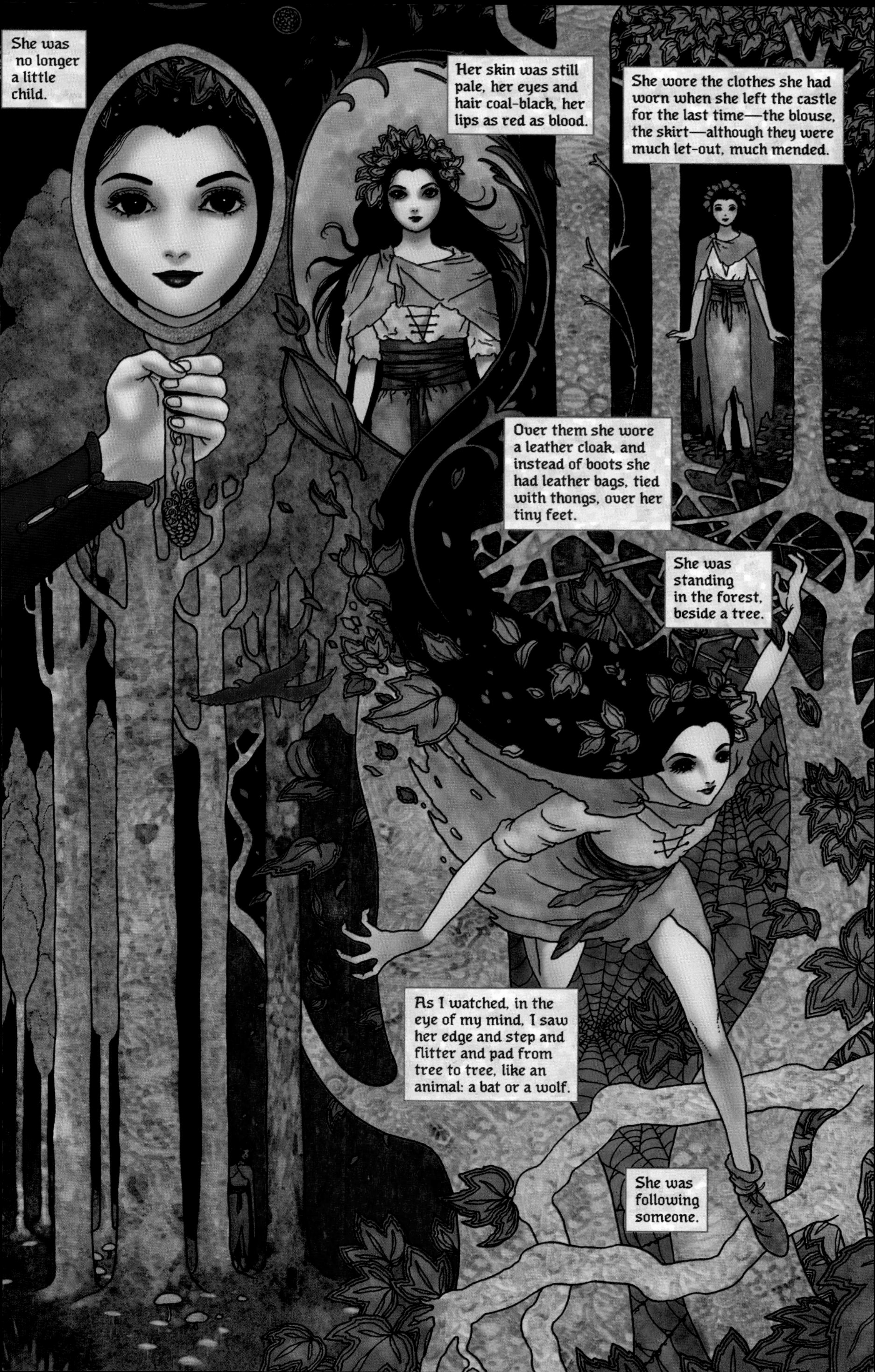
She was no longer a little child.
Her skin was still pale, her eyes and hair coal-black, her lips as red as blood.
She wore the clothes she had worn when she left the castle for the last time—the blouse, the skirt—although they were much let-out, much mended.
Over them she wore a leather cloak, and instead of boots she had leather bags, tied with thongs, over her tiny feet.
She was standing in the forest, beside a tree.
As I watched, in the eye of my mind, I saw her edge and step and flitter and pad from tree to tree, like an animal: a bat or a wolf.
She was following someone.

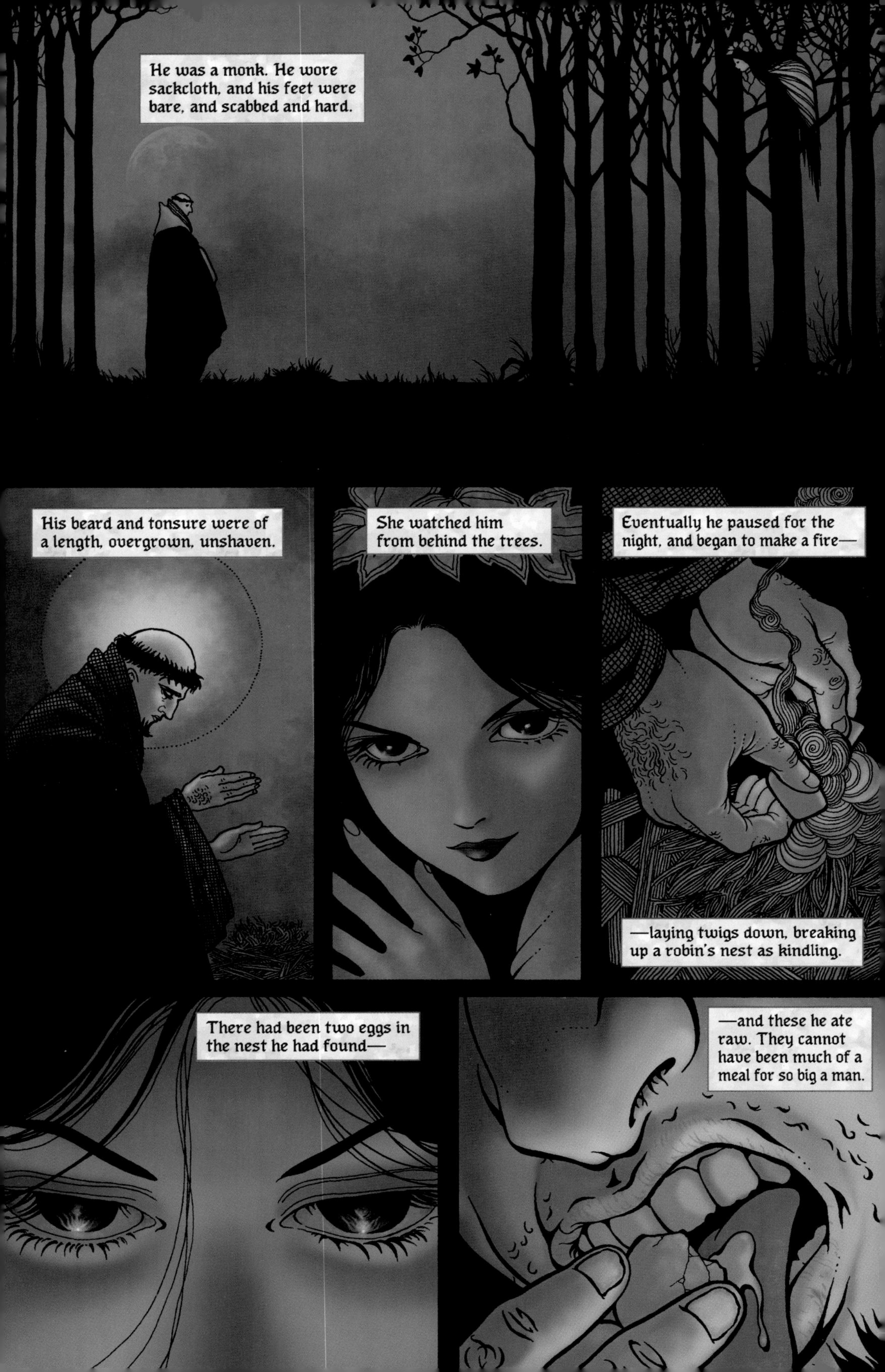
He was a monk. He wore sackcloth, and his feet were bare, and scabbed and hard.
His beard and tonsure were of a length, overgrown, unshaven.
She watched him from behind the trees.
Eventually he paused for the night, and began to make a fire—
—laying twigs down, breaking up a robin's nest as kindling.
There had been two eggs in the nest he had found—
—and these he ate raw. They cannot have been much of a meal for so big a man.

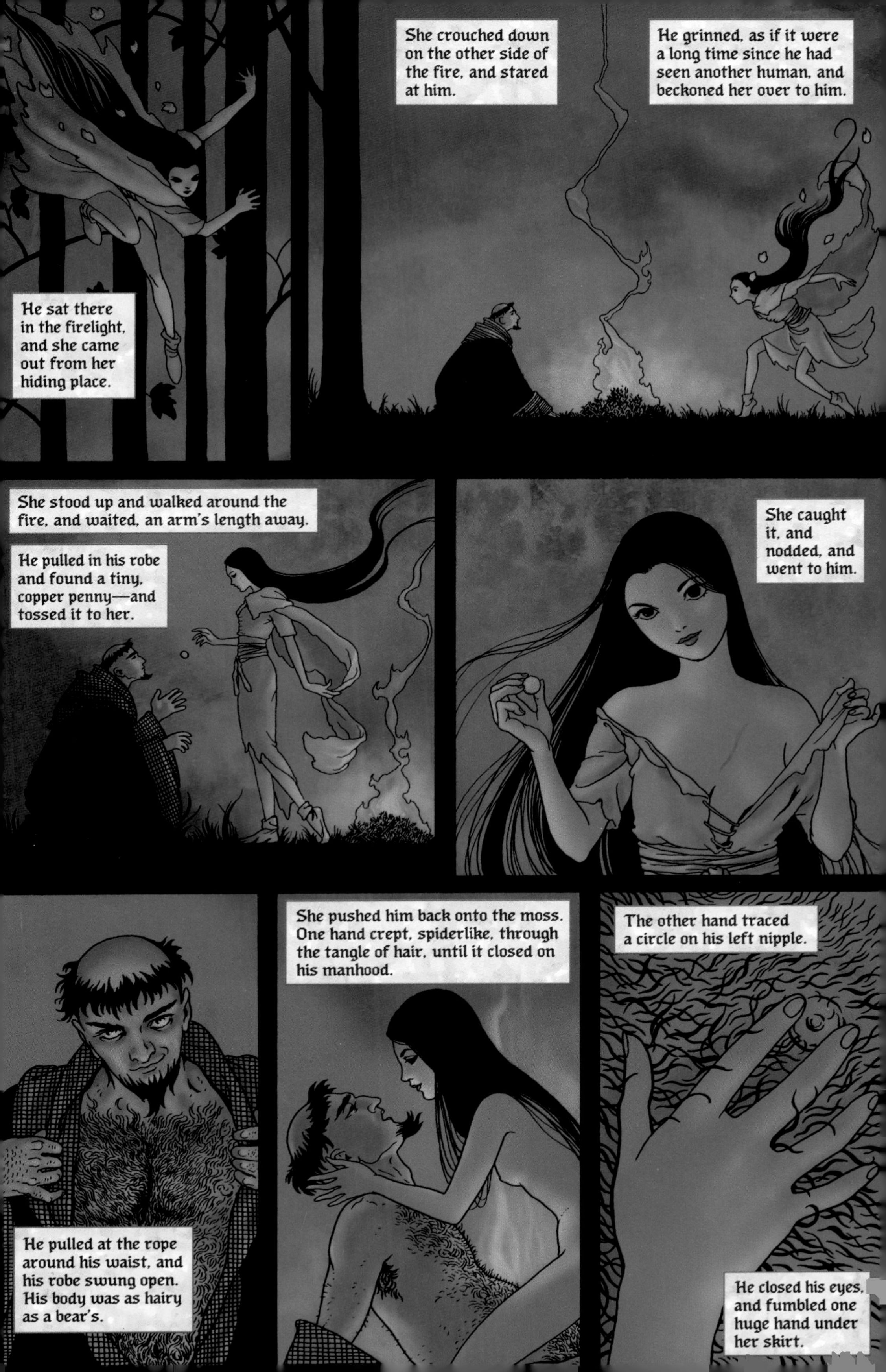
He sat there in the firelight, and she came out from her hiding place.
She crouched down on the other side of the fire, and stared at him.
He grinned, as if it were a long time since he had seen another human, and beckoned her over to him.
She stood up and walked around the fire, and waited, an arm's length away.
He pulled in his robe and found a tiny, copper penny—and tossed it to her.
She caught it, and nodded, and went to him.
He pulled at the rope around his waist, and his robe swung open. His body was as hairy as a bear's.
She pushed him back onto the moss. One hand crept, spiderlike, through the tangle of hair, until it closed on his manhood.
The other hand traced a circle on his left nipple.
He closed his eyes, and fumbled one huge hand under her skirt.

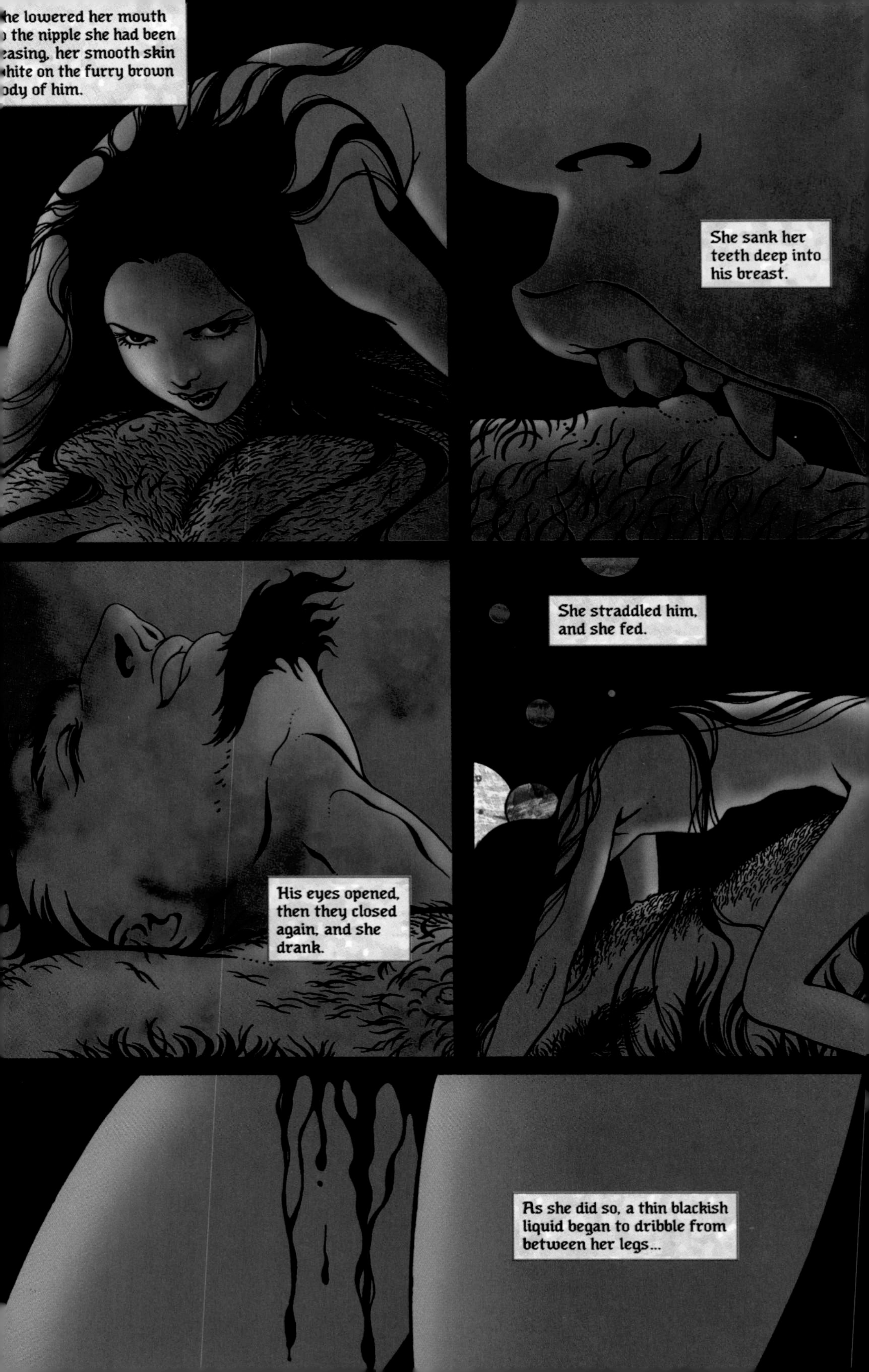
he lowered her mouth the nipple she had been easing, her smooth skin hite on the furry brown ody of him.
She sank her teeth deep into his breast.
His eyes opened, then they closed again, and she drank.
She straddled him, and she fed.
As she did so, a thin blackish liquid began to dribble from between her legs...

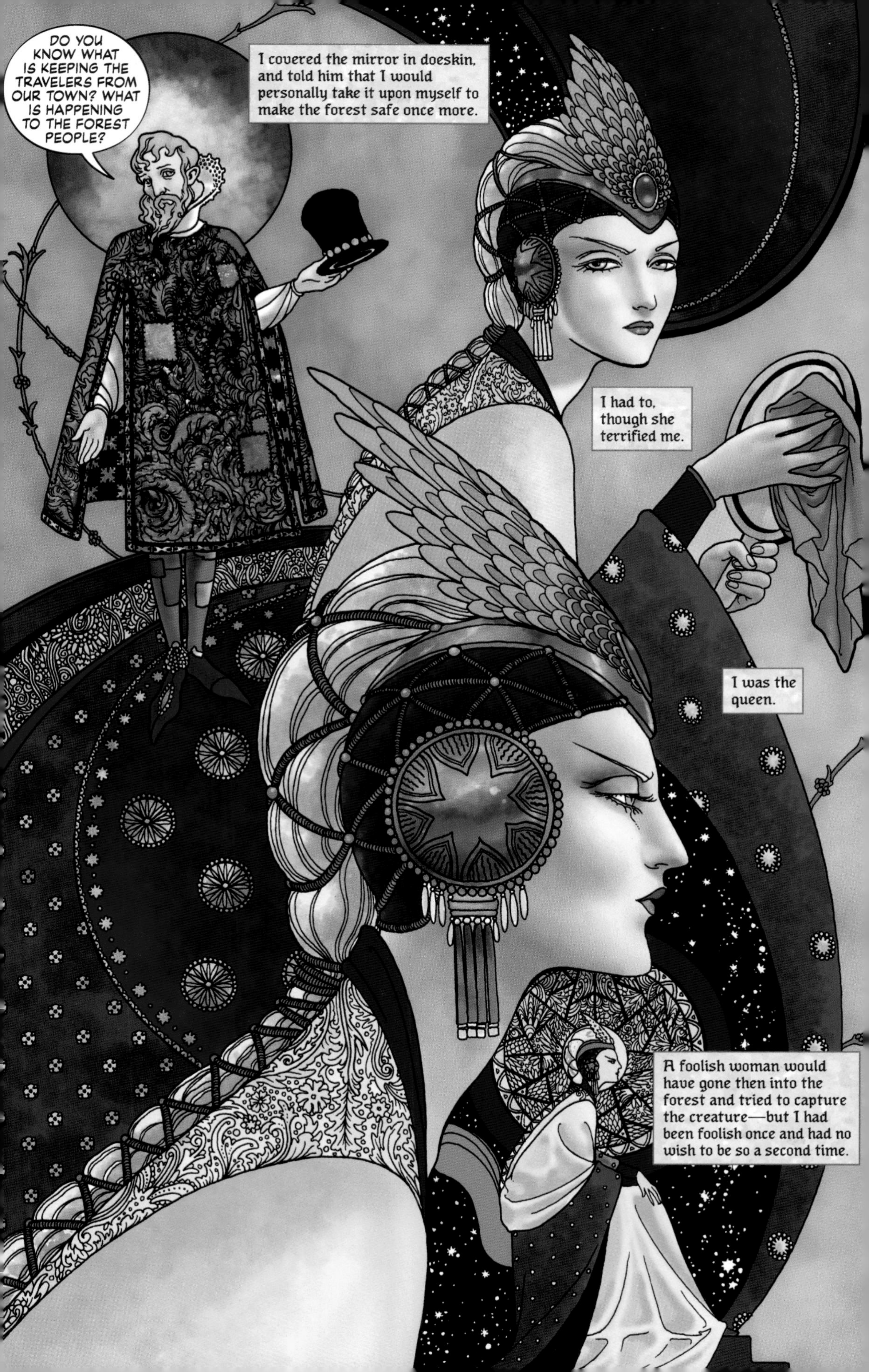
DO YOU KNOW WHAT IS KEEPING THE TRAVELERS FROM OUR TOWN? WHAT IS HAPPENING TO THE FOREST PEOPLE?
I covered the mirror in doeskin, and told him that I would personally take it upon myself to make the forest safe once more.
I had to, though she terrified me.
I was the queen.
A foolish woman would have gone then into the forest and tried to capture the creature—but I had been foolish once and had no wish to be so a second time.

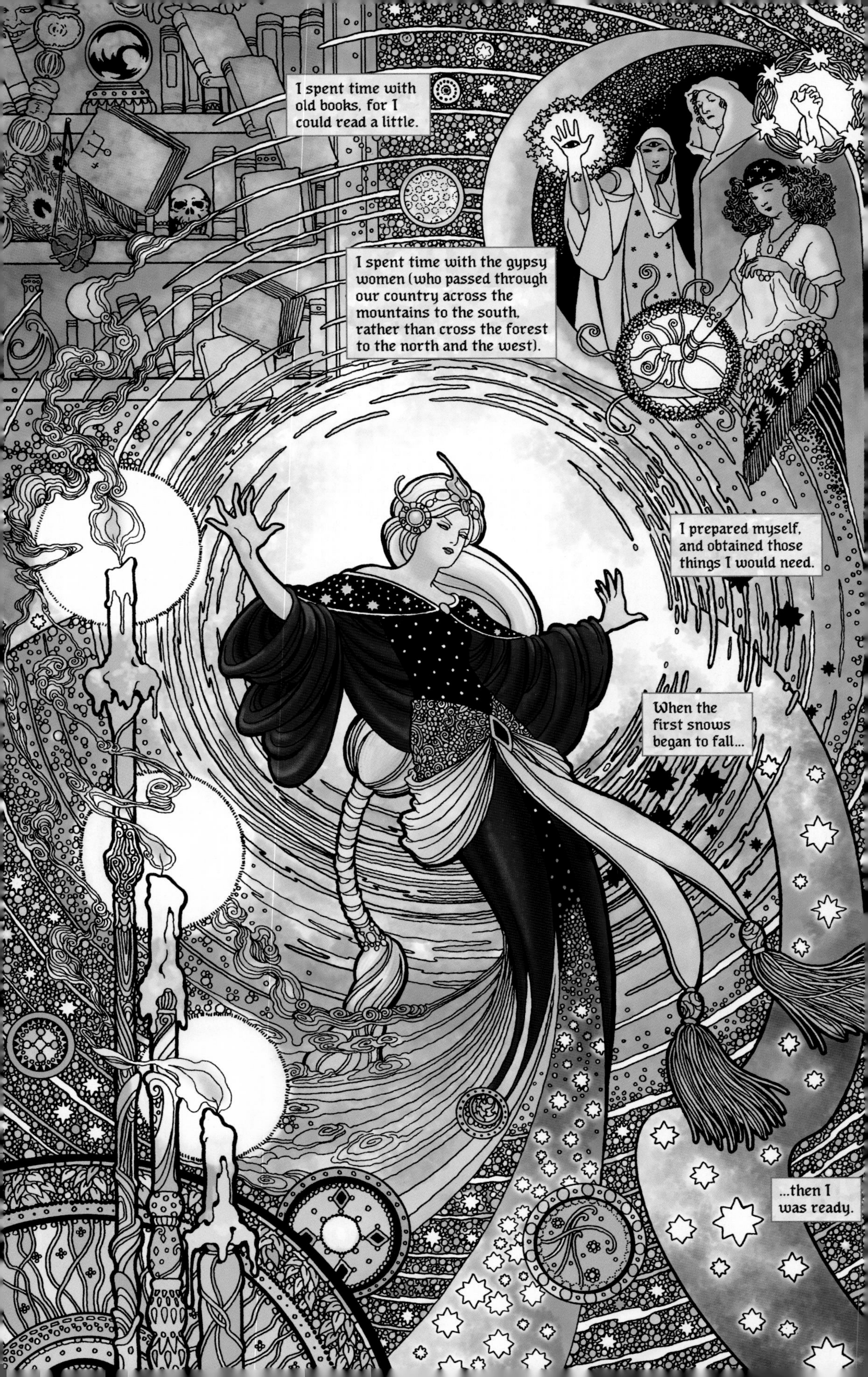
I spent time with old books, for I could read a little.
I spent time with the gypsy women (who passed through our country across the mountains to the south, rather than cross the forest to the north and the west).
I prepared myself, and obtained those things I would need.
When the first snows began to fall...
...then I was ready.

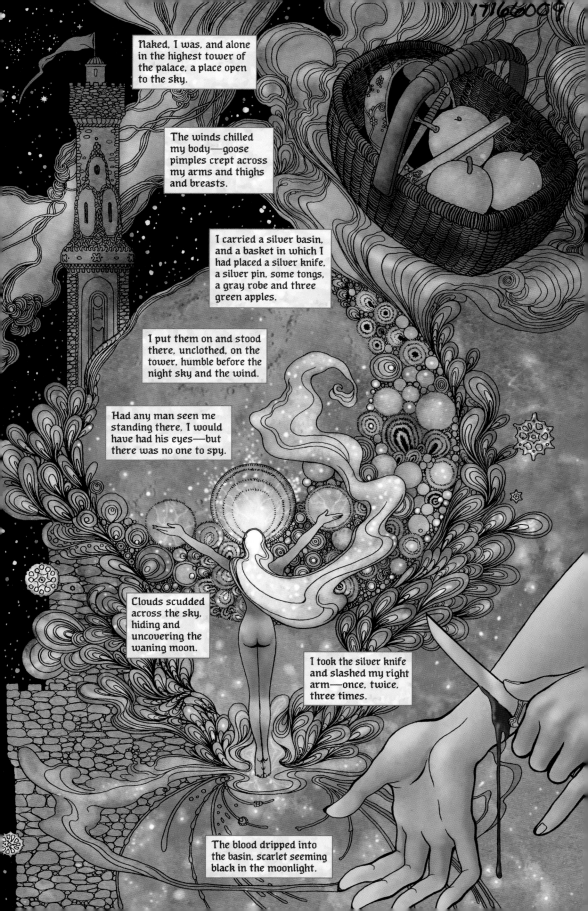

Naked, I was, and alone in the highest tower of the palace, a place open to the sky.

The winds chilled my body—goose pimples crept across my arms and thighs and breasts.

I carried a silver basin, and a basket in which I had placed a silver knife, a silver pin, some tongs, a gray robe and three green apples.

I put them on and stood there, unclothed, on the tower, humble before the night sky and the wind.

Had any man seen me standing there, I would have had his eyes—but there was no one to spy.

Clouds scudded across the sky, hiding and uncovering the waning moon.

I took the silver knife and slashed my right arm—once, twice, three times.

The blood dripped into the basin, scarlet seeming black in the moonlight.

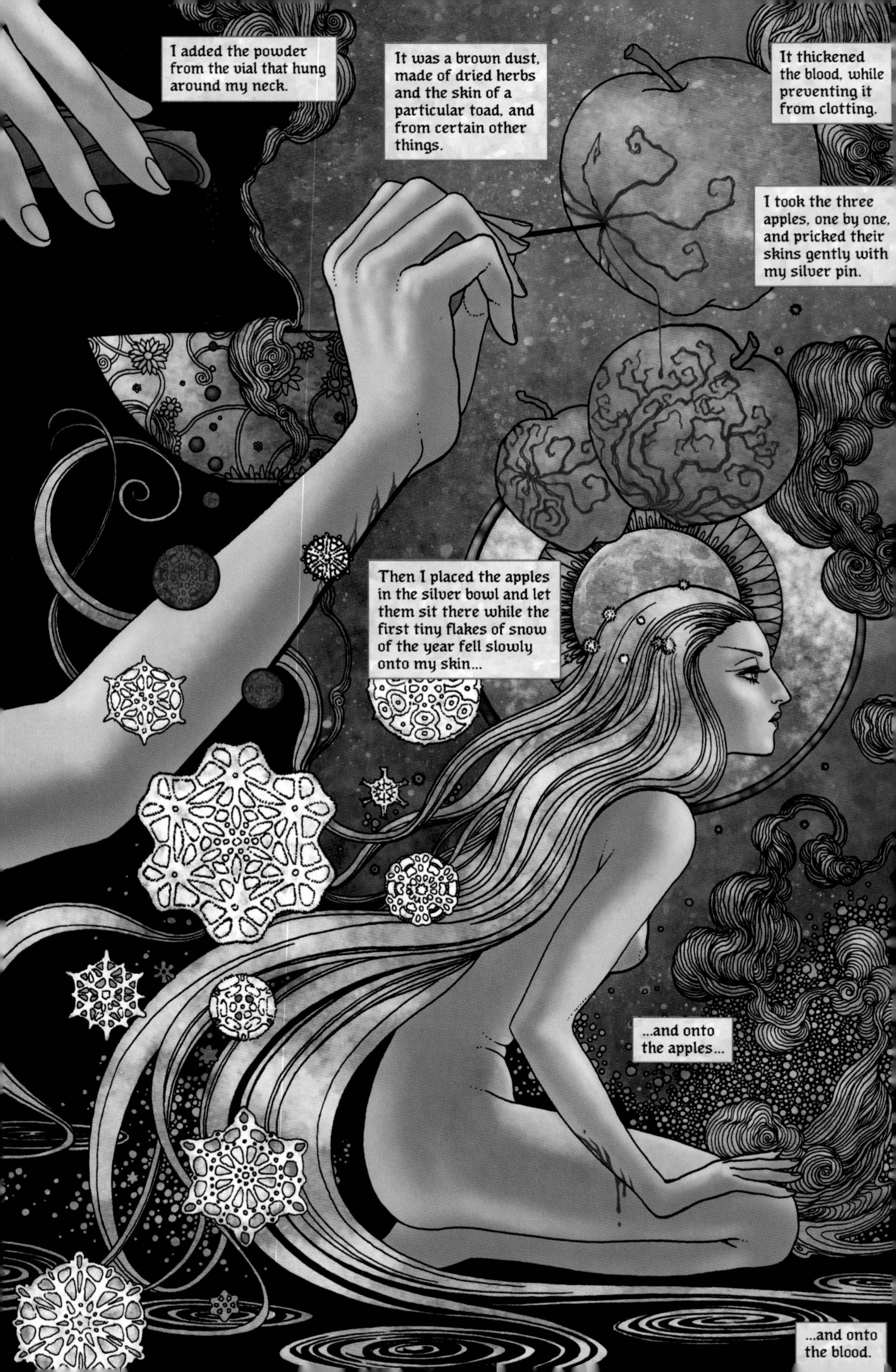
I added the powder from the vial that hung around my neck.
It was a brown dust, made of dried herbs and the skin of a particular toad, and from certain other things.
It thickened the blood, while preventing it from clotting.
I took the three apples, one by one, and pricked their skins gently with my silver pin.
Then I placed the apples in the silver bowl and let them sit there while the first tiny flakes of snow of the year fell slowly onto my skin...
...and onto the apples...
...and onto the blood.

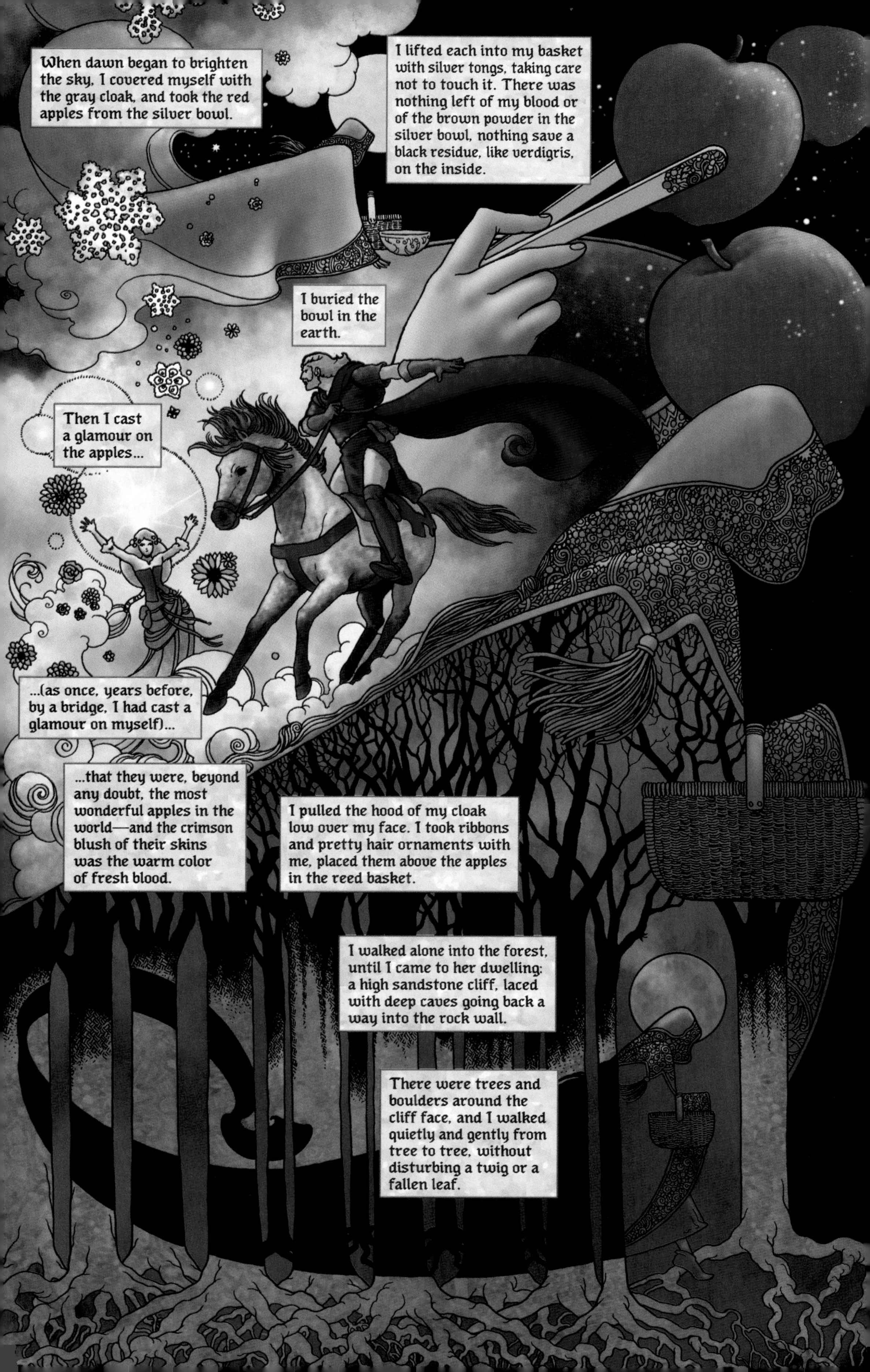

When dawn began to brighten the sky, I covered myself with the gray cloak, and took the red apples from the silver bowl.
I lifted each into my basket with silver tongs, taking care not to touch it. There was nothing left of my blood or of the brown powder in the silver bowl, nothing save a black residue, like verdigris, on the inside.
I buried the bowl in the earth.
Then I cast a glamour on the apples...
...(as once, years before, by a bridge, I had cast a glamour on myself)...
...that they were, beyond any doubt, the most wonderful apples in the world—and the crimson blush of their skins was the warm color of fresh blood.
I pulled the hood of my cloak low over my face. I took ribbons and pretty hair ornaments with me, placed them above the apples in the reed basket.
I walked alone into the forest, until I came to her dwelling: a high sandstone cliff, laced with deep caves going back a way into the rock wall.
There were trees and boulders around the cliff face, and I walked quietly and gently from tree to tree, without disturbing a twig or a fallen leaf.

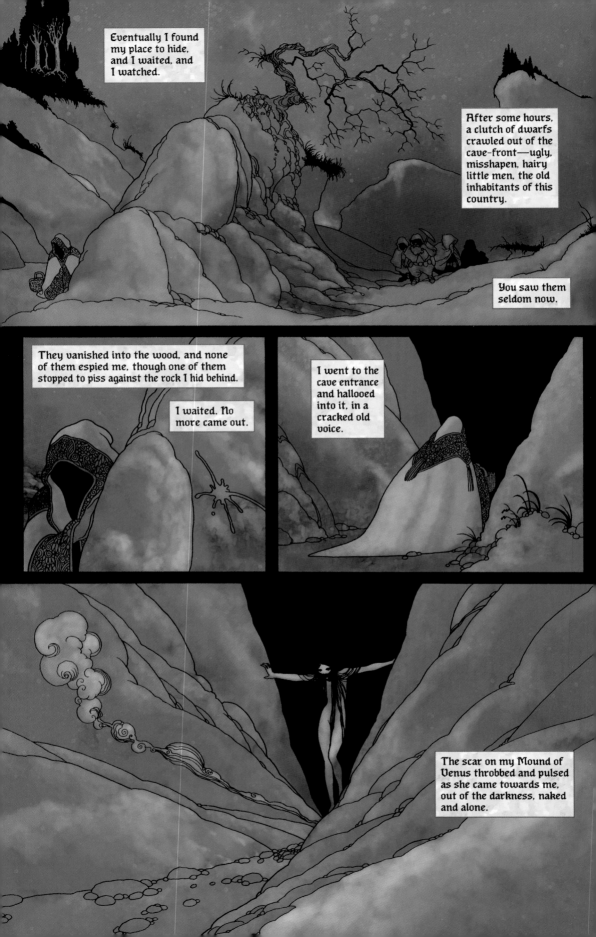

Eventually I found my place to hide, and I waited, and I watched.

After some hours, a clutch of dwarfs crawled out of the cave-front—ugly, misshapen, hairy little men, the old inhabitants of this country.

You saw them seldom now.

They vanished into the wood, and none of them espied me, though one of them stopped to piss against the rock I hid behind.

I waited. No more came out.

I went to the cave entrance and hallooed into it, in a cracked old voice.

The scar on my Mound of Venus throbbed and pulsed as she came towards me, out of the darkness, naked and alone.

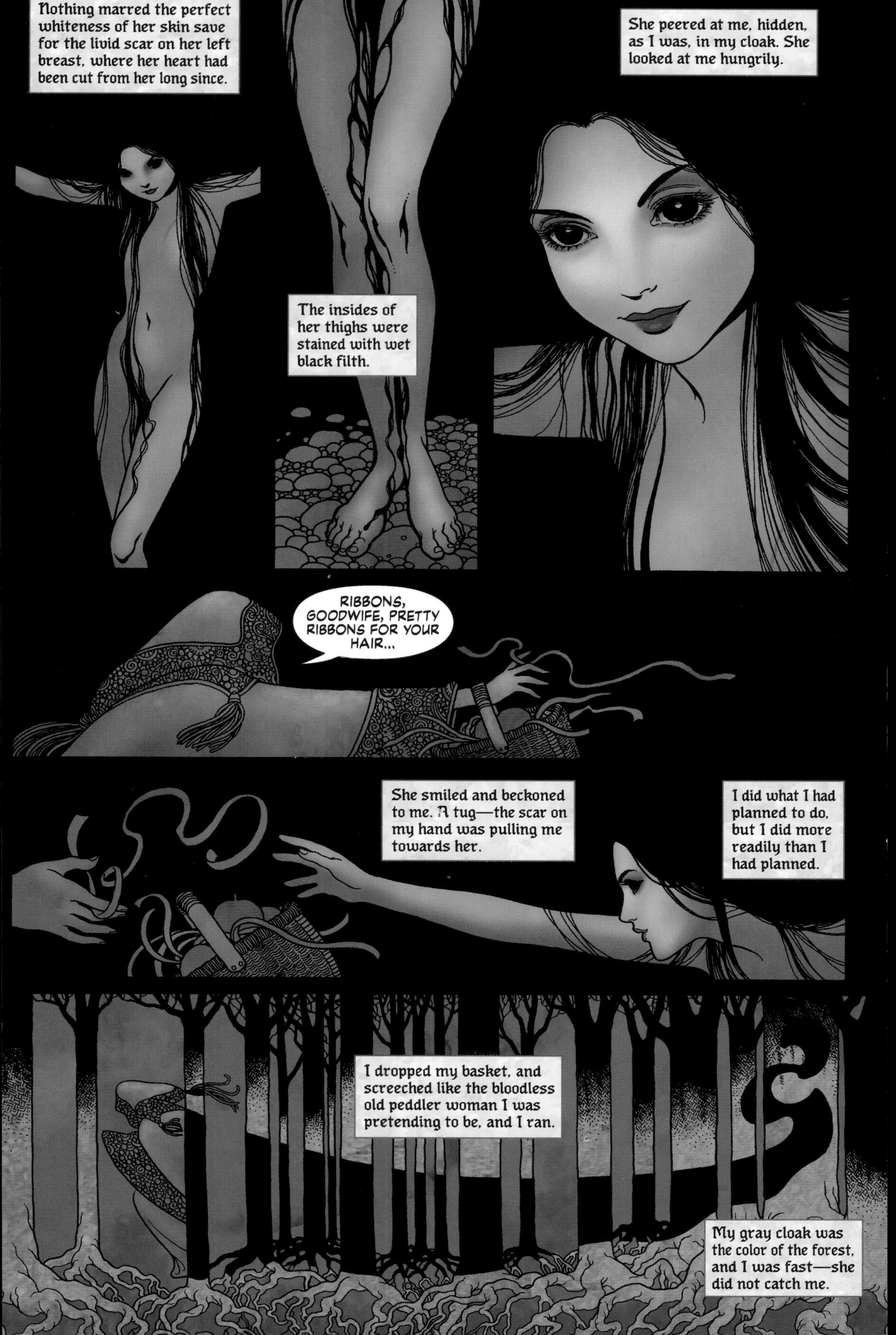

Nothing marred the perfect whiteness of her skin save for the livid scar on her left breast, where her heart had been cut from her long since.
The insides of her thighs were stained with wet black filth.
She peered at me, hidden, as I was, in my cloak. She looked at me hungrily.
RIBBONS, GOODWIFE, PRETTY RIBBONS FOR YOUR HAIR...
She smiled and beckoned to me. A tug—the scar on my hand was pulling me towards her.
I did what I had planned to do, but I did more readily than I had planned.
I dropped my basket, and screeched like the bloodless old peddler woman I was pretending to be, and I ran.
My gray cloak was the color of the forest, and I was fast—she did not catch me.

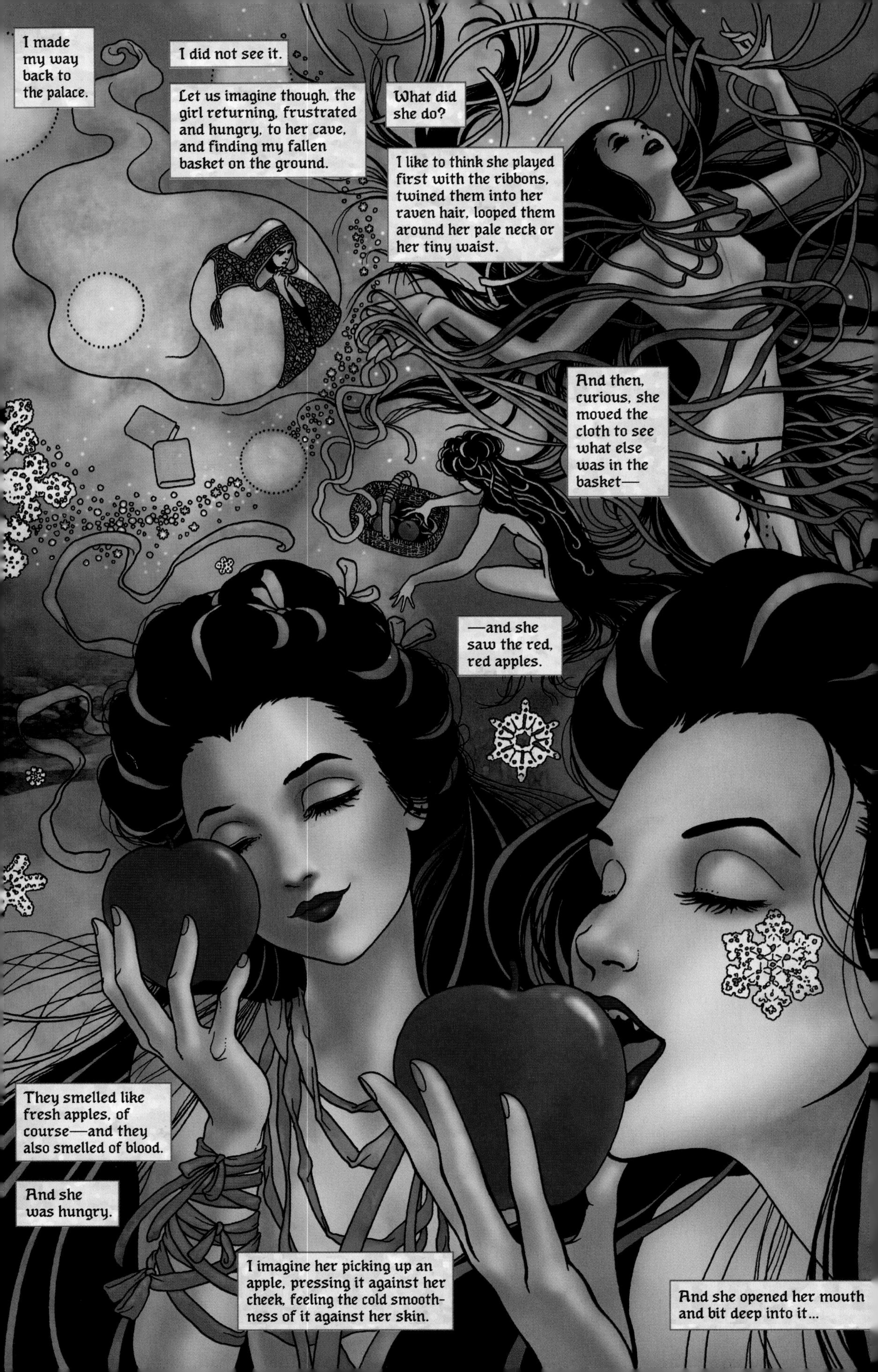

I made my way back to the palace.
I did not see it.
Let us imagine though, the girl returning, frustrated and hungry, to her cave, and finding my fallen basket on the ground.
What did she do?
I like to think she played first with the ribbons, twined them into her raven hair, looped them around her pale neck or her tiny waist.
And then, curious, she moved the cloth to see what else was in the basket—
—and she saw the red, red apples.
They smelled like fresh apples, of course—and they also smelled of blood.
And she was hungry.
I imagine her picking up an apple, pressing it against her cheek, feeling the cold smoothness of it against her skin.
And she opened her mouth and bit deep into it...

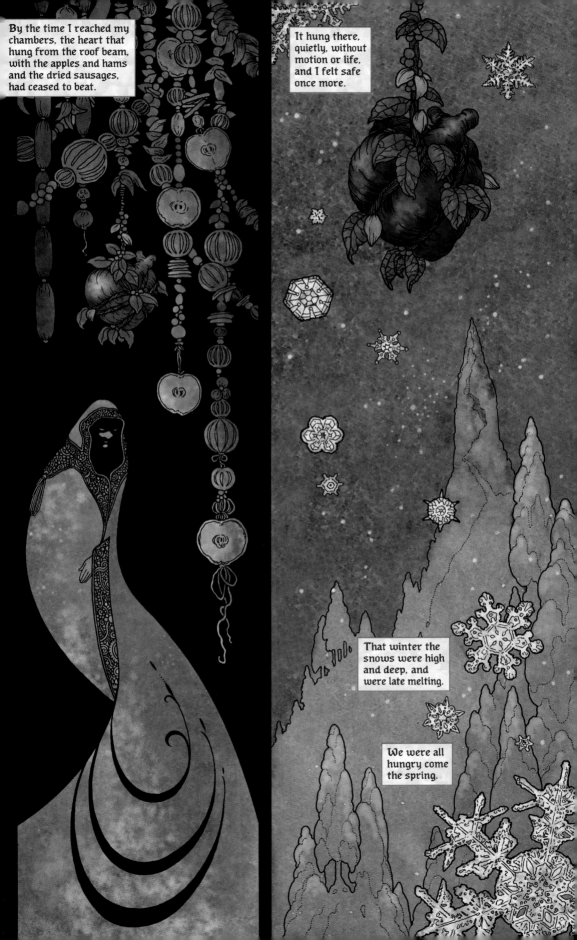

By the time I reached my chambers, the heart that hung from the roof beam, with the apples and hams and the dried sausages, had ceased to beat.

It hung there, quietly, without motion or life, and I felt safe once more.

That winter the snows were high and deep, and were late melting.

We were all hungry come the spring.

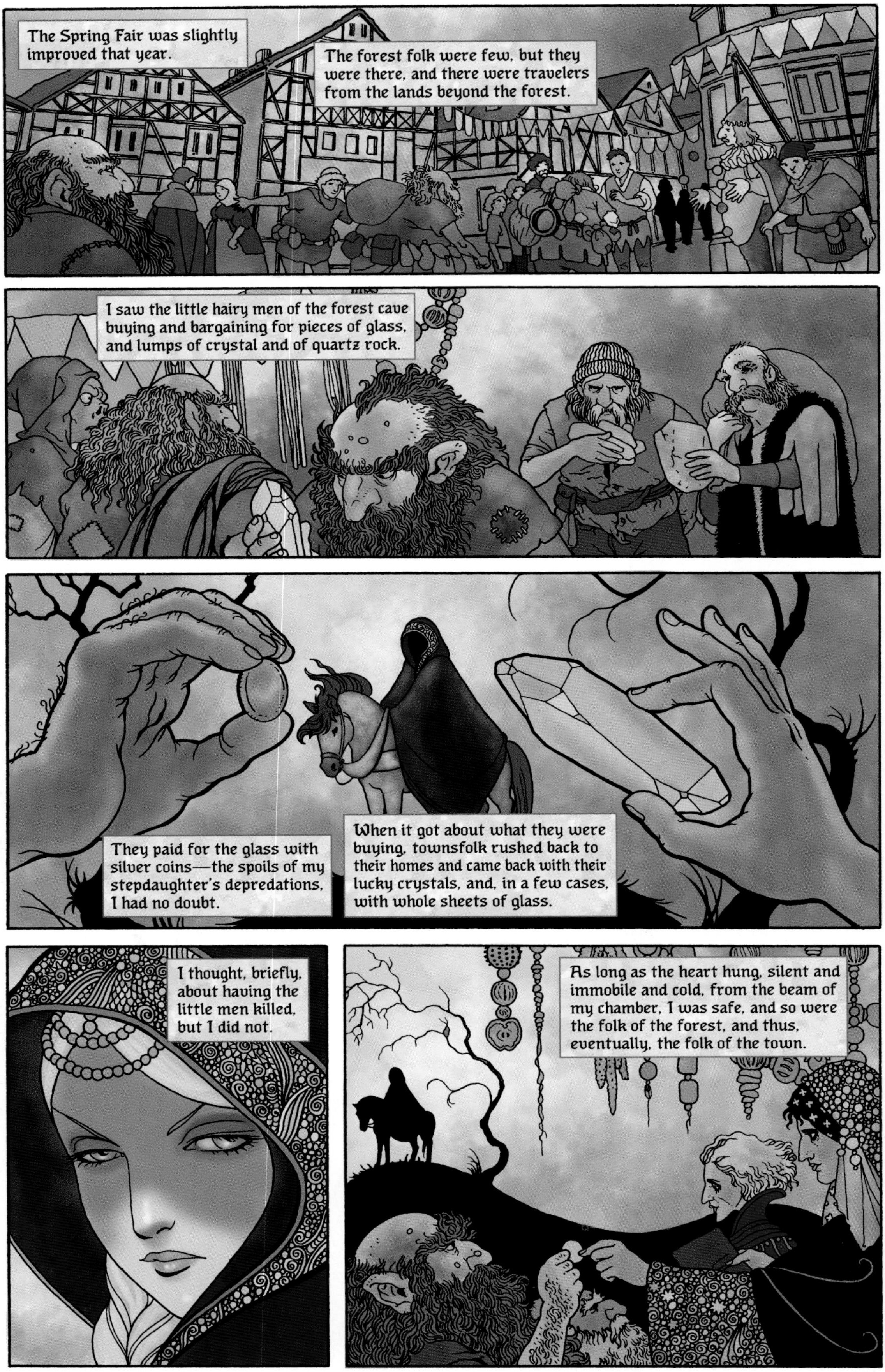
The Spring Fair was slightly improved that year.
The forest folk were few, but they were there, and there were travelers from the lands beyond the forest.
I saw the little hairy men of the forest cave buying and bargaining for pieces of glass, and lumps of crystal and of quartz rock.
They paid for the glass with silver coins—the spoils of my stepdaughter's depredations, I had no doubt.
When it got about what they were buying, townsfolk rushed back to their homes and came back with their lucky crystals, and, in a few cases, with whole sheets of glass.
I thought, briefly, about having the little men killed, but I did not.
As long as the heart hung, silent and immobile and cold, from the beam of my chamber, I was safe, and so were the folk of the forest, and thus, eventually, the folk of the town.

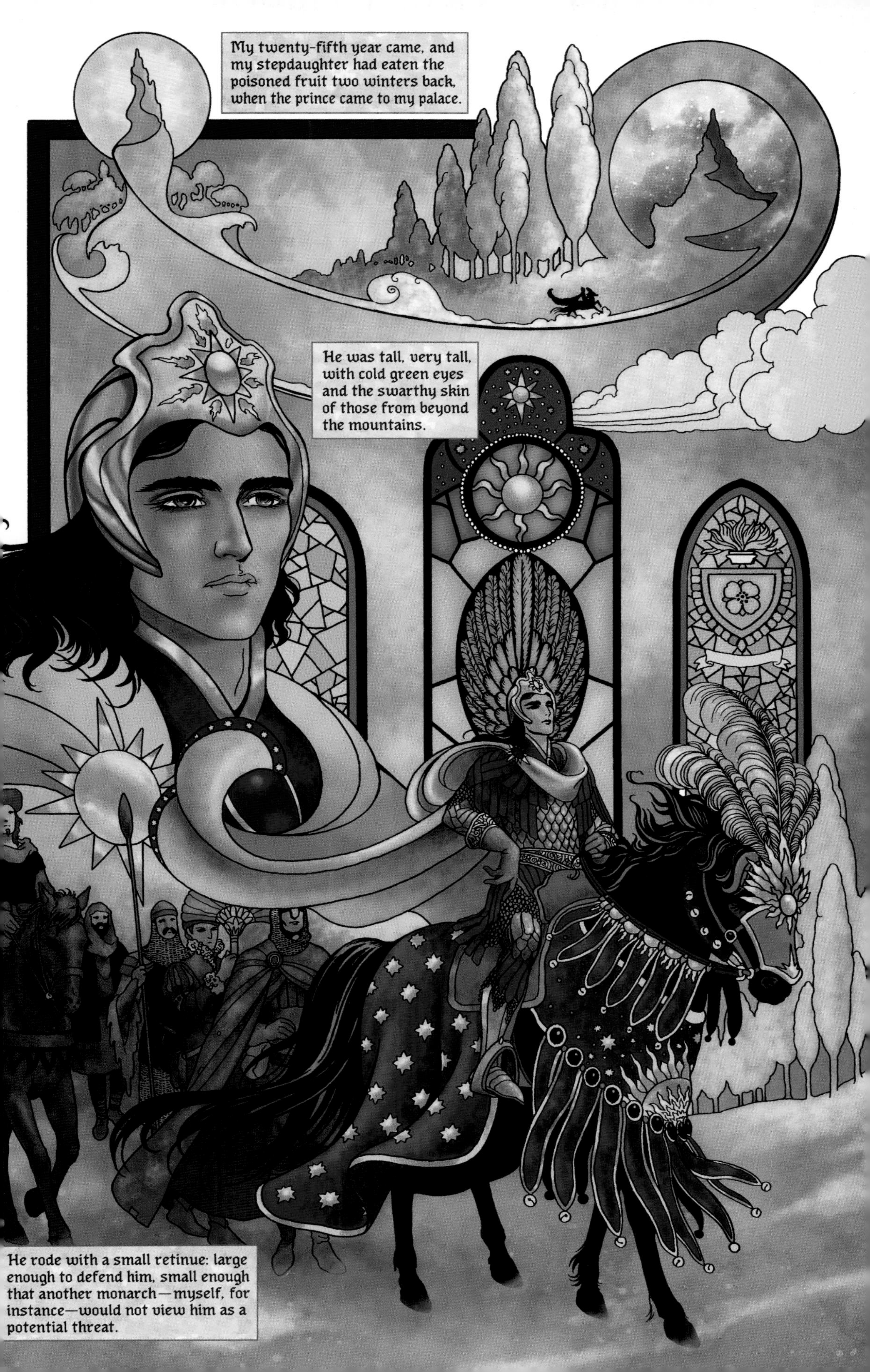
My twenty-fifth year came, and my stepdaughter had eaten the poisoned fruit two winters back, when the prince came to my palace.
He was tall, very tall, with cold green eyes and the swarthy skin of those from beyond the mountains.
He rode with a small retinue: large enough to defend him, small enough that another monarch—myself, for instance—would not view him as a potential threat.

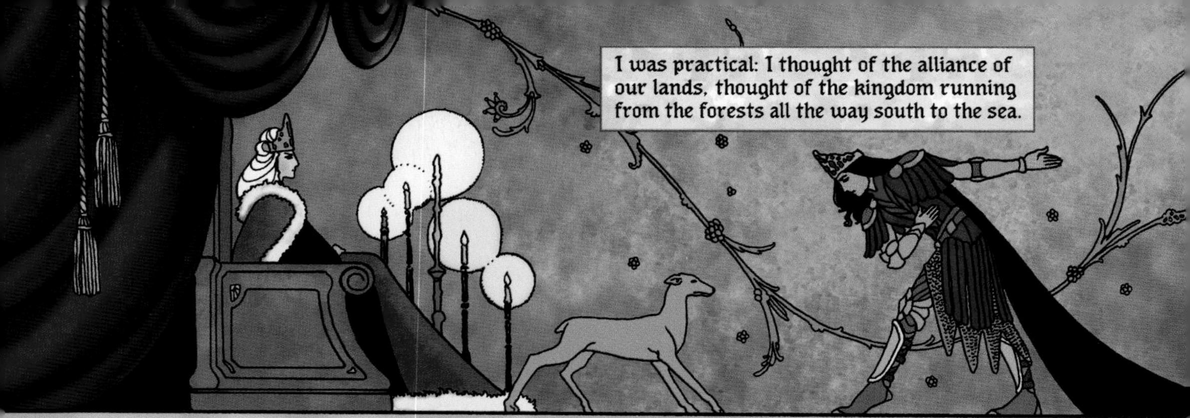
I was practical: I thought of the alliance of our lands, thought of the kingdom running from the forests all the way south to the sea.

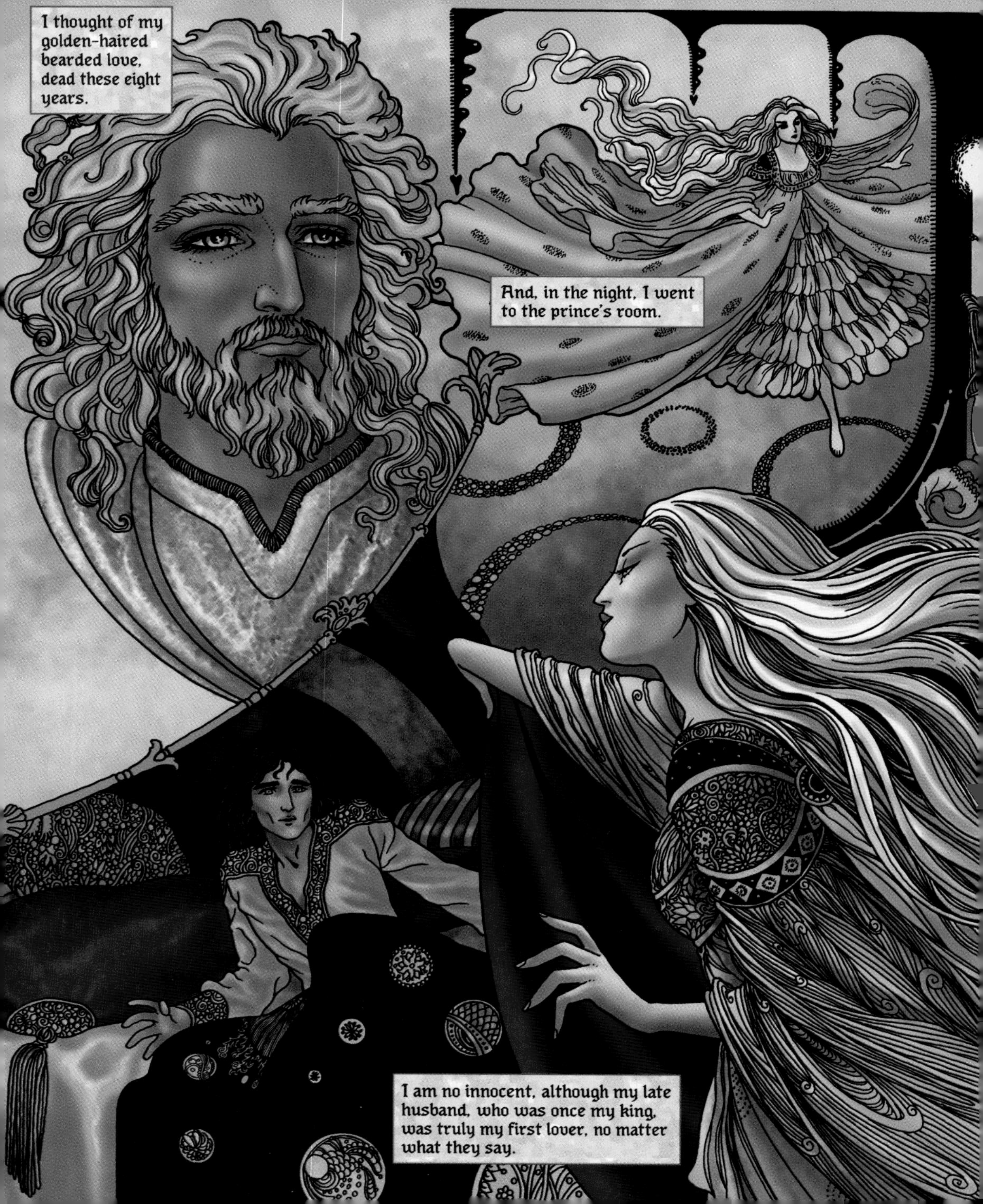
I thought of my golden-haired bearded love, dead these eight years.
And, in the night, I went to the prince's room.
I am no innocent, although my late husband, who was once my king, was truly my first lover, no matter what they say.

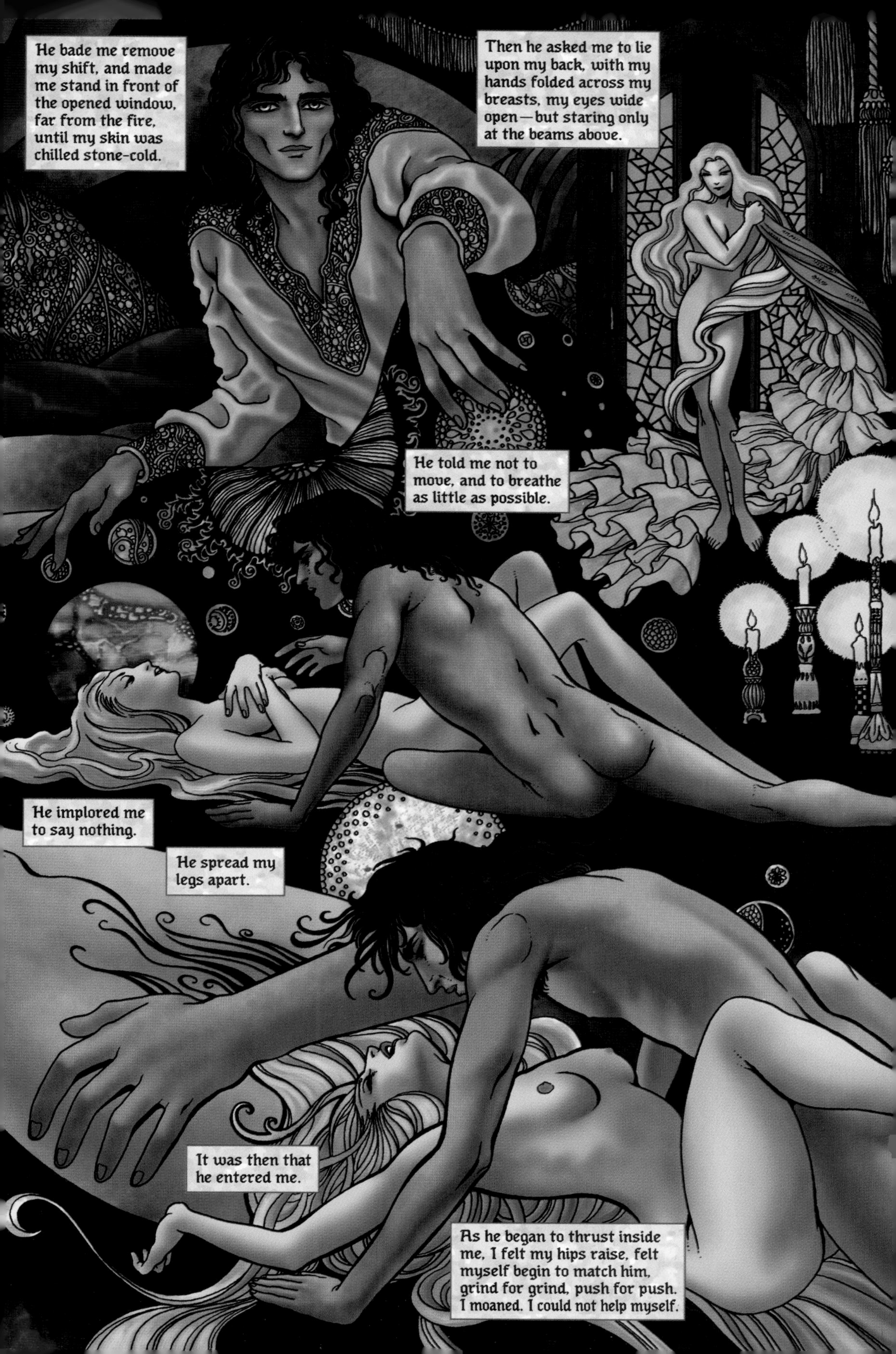
He bade me remove my shift, and made me stand in front of the opened window, far from the fire, until my skin was chilled stone-cold.
Then he asked me to lie upon my back, with my hands folded across my breasts, my eyes wide open—but staring only at the beams above.
He told me not to move, and to breathe as little as possible.
He implored me to say nothing.
He spread my legs apart.
It was then that he entered me.
As he began to thrust inside me, I felt my hips raise, felt myself begin to match him, grind for grind, push for push. I moaned. I could not help myself.

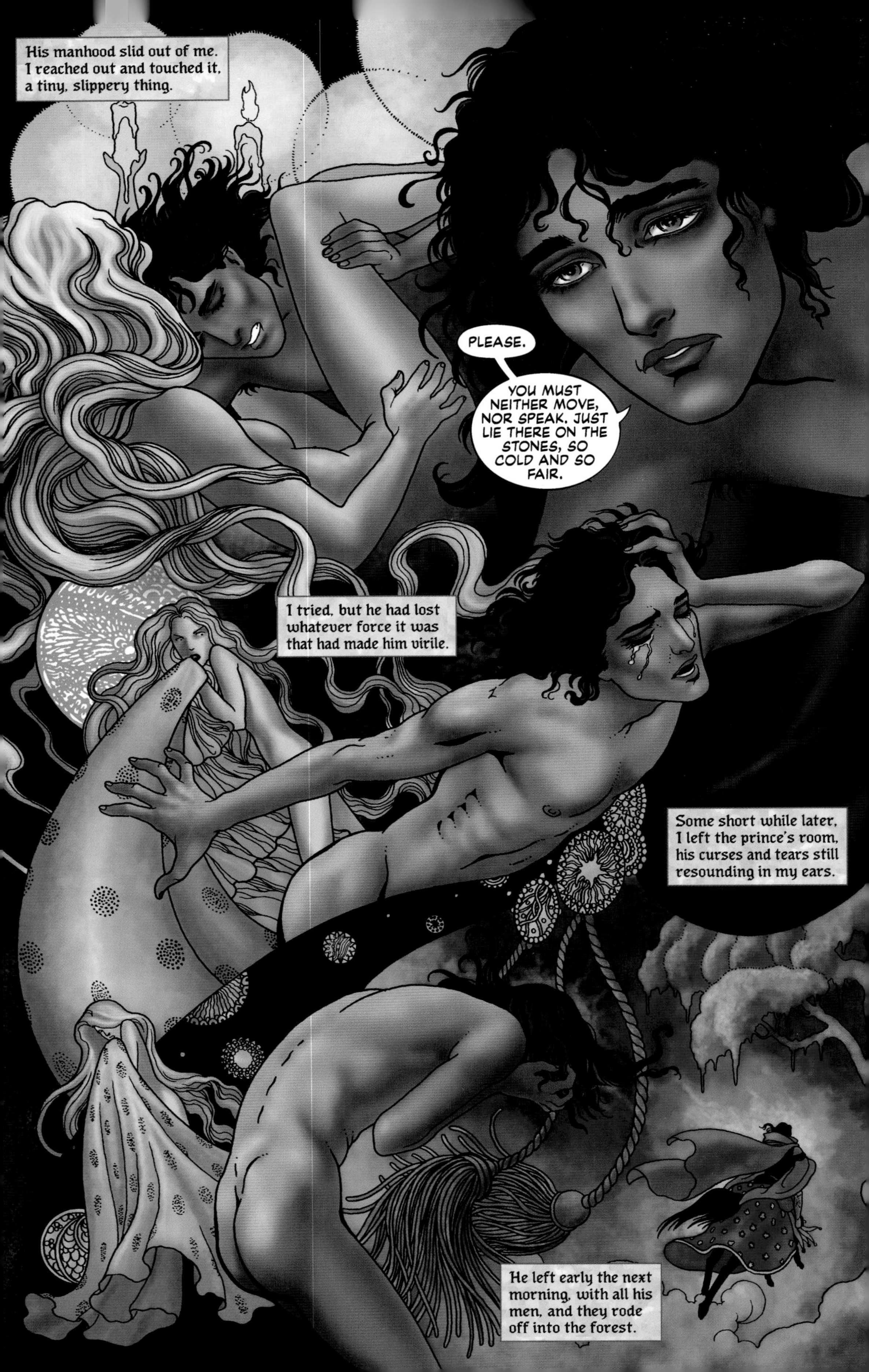
His manhood slid out of me. I reached out and touched it, a tiny, slippery thing.
PLEASE.
YOU MUST NEITHER MOVE, NOR SPEAK. JUST LIE THERE ON THE STONES, SO COLD AND SO FAIR.
I tried, but he had lost whatever force it was that had made him virile.
Some short while later, I left the prince's room, his curses and tears still resounding in my ears.
He left early the next morning, with all his men, and they rode off into the forest.

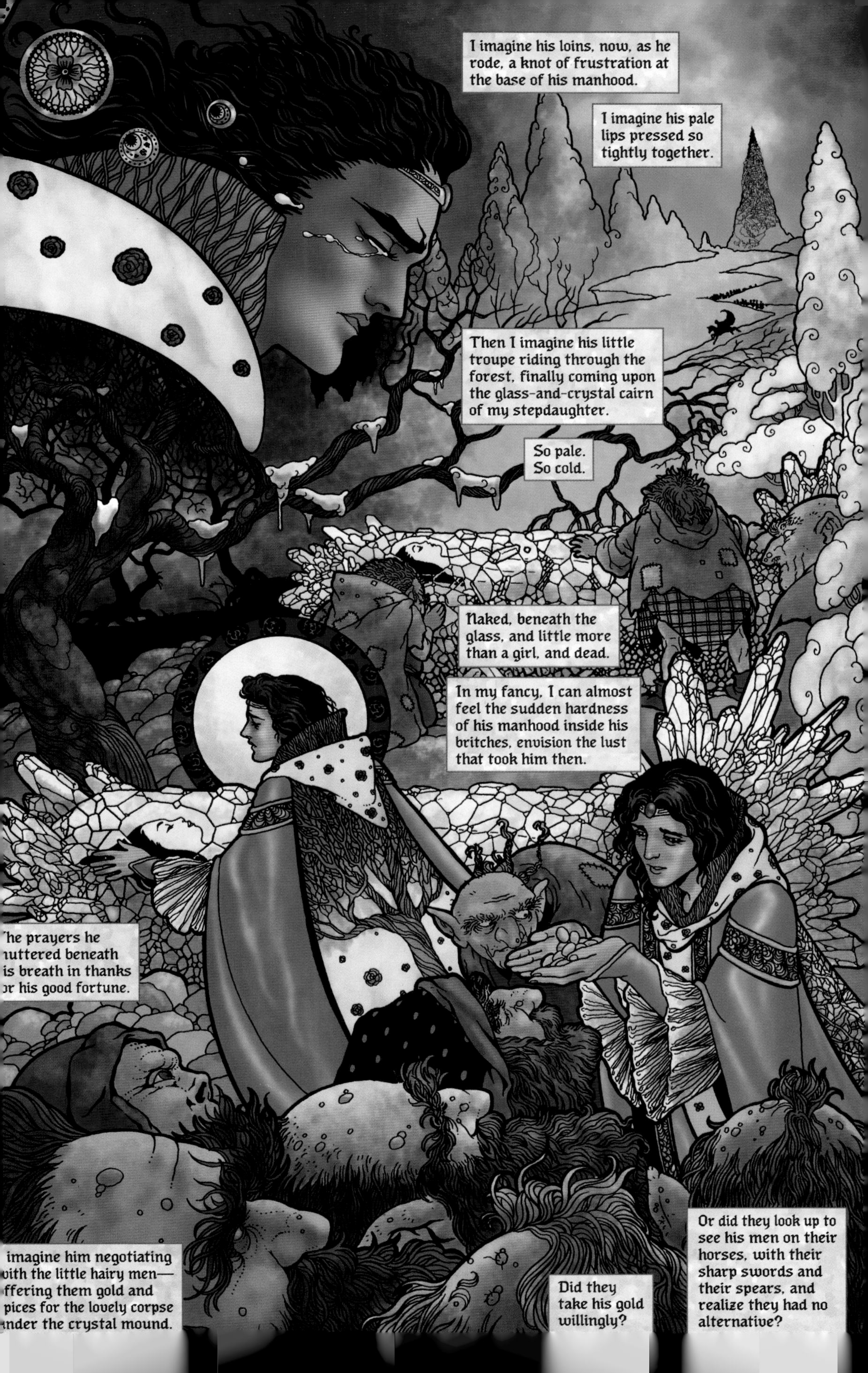

I imagine his loins, now, as he rode, a knot of frustration at the base of his manhood.
I imagine his pale lips pressed so tightly together.
Then I imagine his little troupe riding through the forest, finally coming upon the glass-and-crystal cairn of my stepdaughter.
So pale. So cold.
Naked, beneath the glass, and little more than a girl, and dead.
In my fancy, I can almost feel the sudden hardness of his manhood inside his britches, envision the lust that took him then.
he prayers he uttered beneath is breath in thanks or his good fortune.
imagine him negotiating with the little hairy men— ffering them gold and pices for the lovely corpse nder the crystal mound.
Did they take his gold willingly?
Or did they look up to see his men on their horses, with their sharp swords and their spears, and realize they had no alternative?

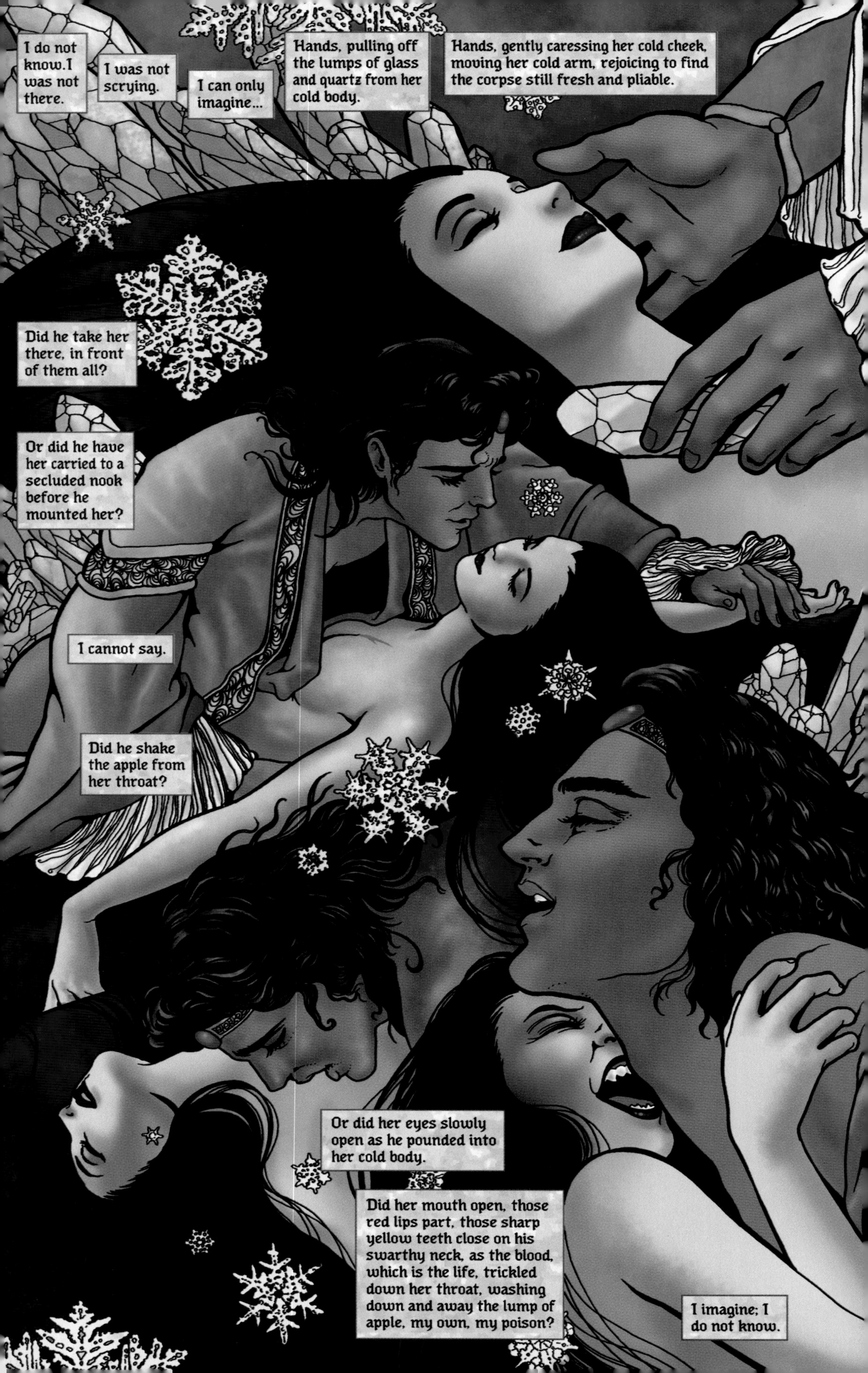
I do not know. I was not there.
I was not scrying.
I can only imagine...
Hands, pulling off the lumps of glass and quartz from her cold body.
Hands, gently caressing her cold cheek, moving her cold arm, rejoicing to find the corpse still fresh and pliable.
Did he take her there, in front of them all?
Or did he have her carried to a secluded nook before he mounted her?
I cannot say.
Did he shake the apple from her throat?
Or did her eyes slowly open as he pounded into her cold body.
Did her mouth open, those red lips part, those sharp yellow teeth close on his swarthy neck, as the blood, which is the life, trickled down her throat, washing down and away the lump of apple, my own, my poison?
I imagine; I do not know.

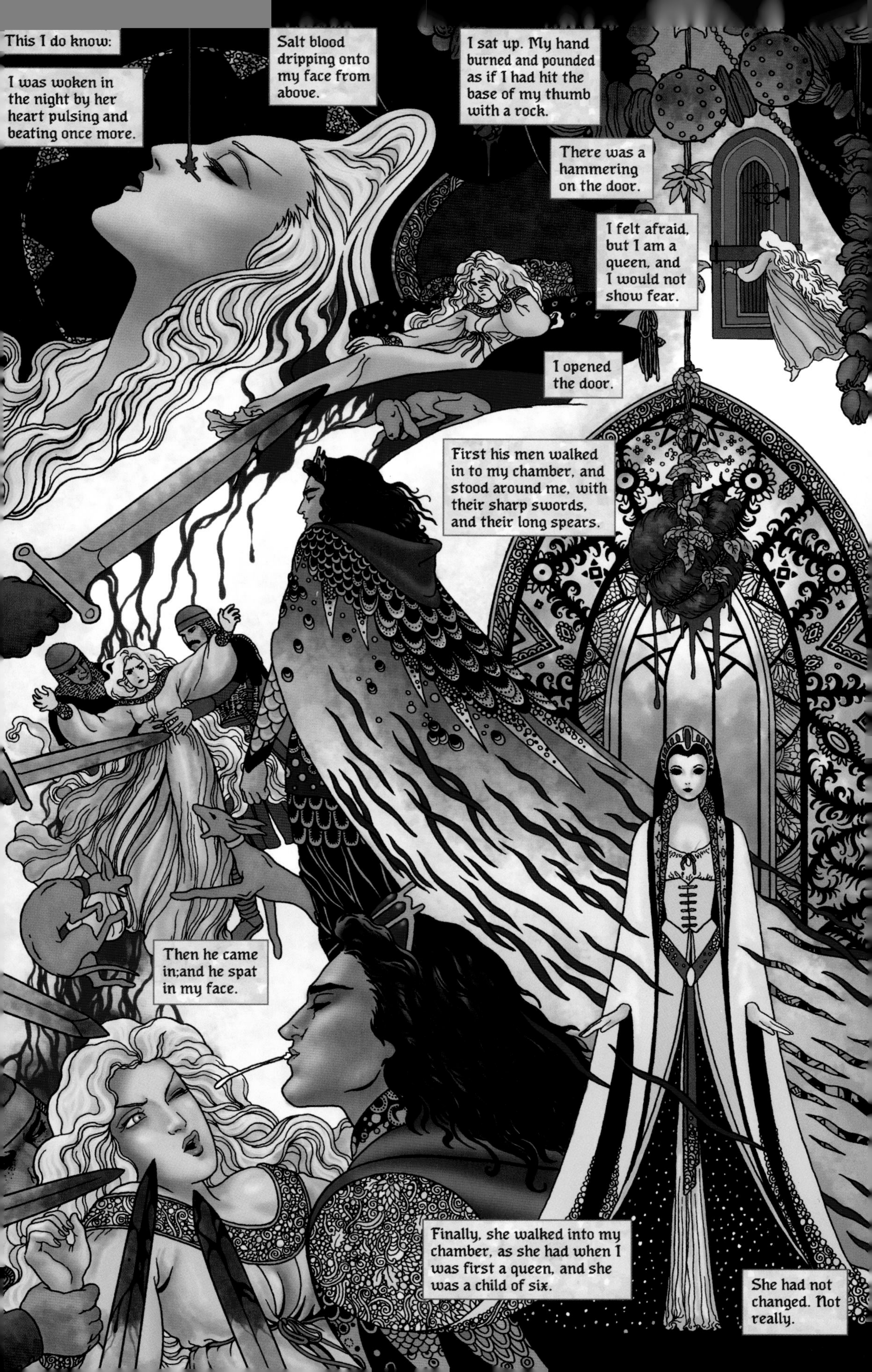
This I do know:
I was woken in the night by her heart pulsing and beating once more.
Salt blood dripping onto my face from above.
I sat up. My hand burned and pounded as if I had hit the base of my thumb with a rock.
There was a hammering on the door.
I felt afraid, but I am a queen, and I would not show fear.
I opened the door.
First his men walked in to my chamber, and stood around me, with their sharp swords, and their long spears.
Then he came in;and he spat in my face.
Finally, she walked into my chamber, as she had when I was first a queen, and she was a child of six.
She had not changed. Not really.

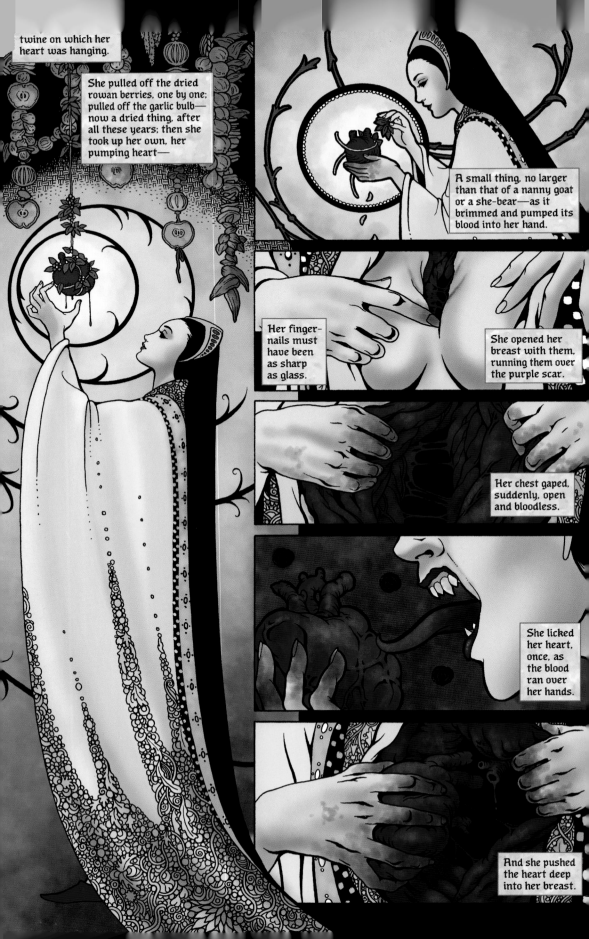

twine on which her heart was hanging.

She pulled off the dried rowan berries, one by one; pulled off the garlic bulb—now a dried thing, after all these years; then she took up her own, her pumping heart—

A small thing, no larger than that of a nanny goat or a she-bear—as it brimmed and pumped its blood into her hand.

Her finger-nails must have been as sharp as glass.

She opened her breast with them, running them over the purple scar.

Her chest gaped, suddenly, open and bloodless.

She licked her heart, once, as the blood ran over her hands.

And she pushed the heart deep into her breast.

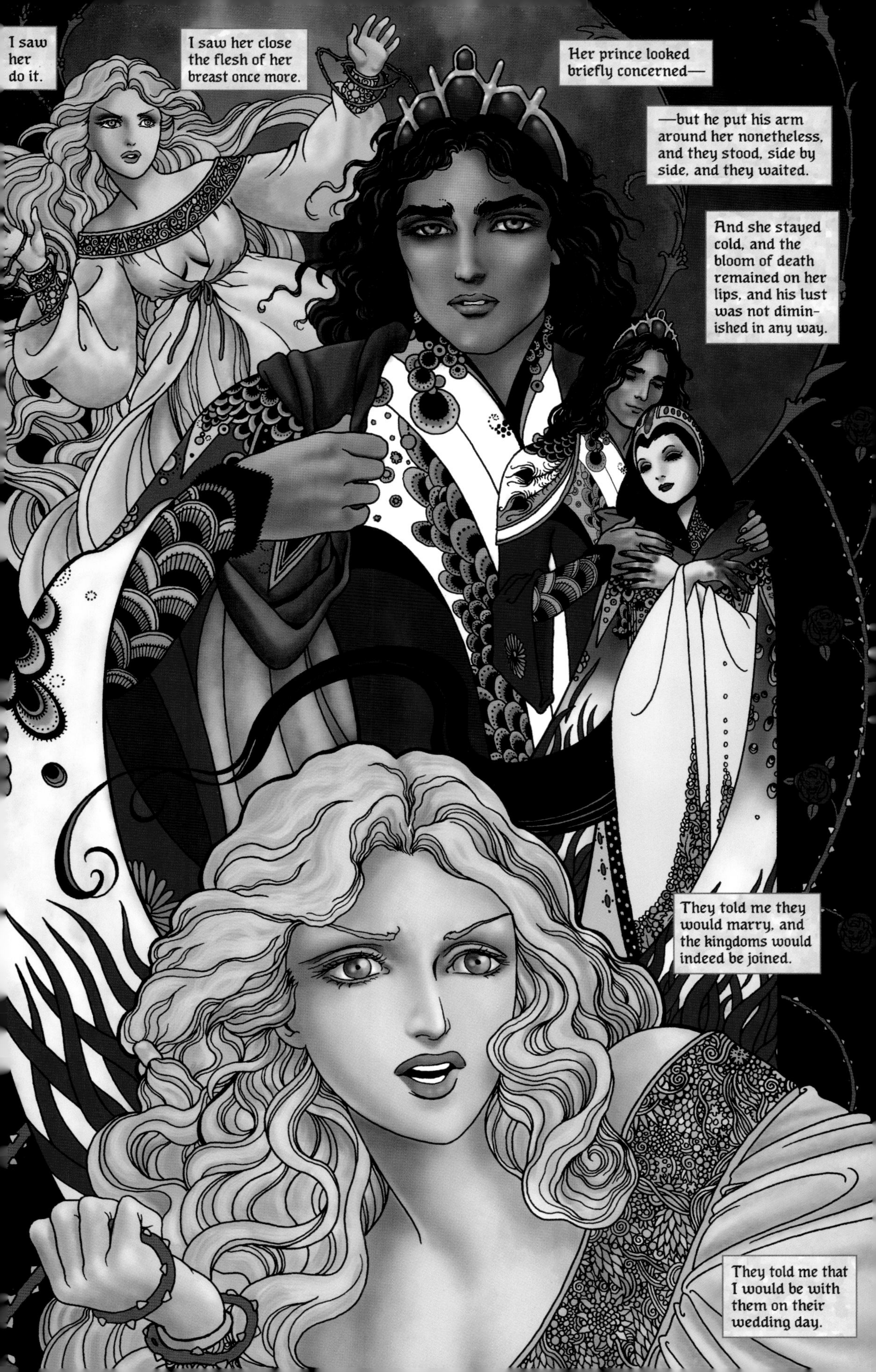
I saw her do it.
I saw her close the flesh of her breast once more.
Her prince looked briefly concerned—
—but he put his arm around her nonetheless, and they stood, side by side, and they waited.
And she stayed cold, and the bloom of death remained on her lips, and his lust was not dimin-ished in any way.
They told me they would marry, and the kingdoms would indeed be joined.
They told me that I would be with them on their wedding day.

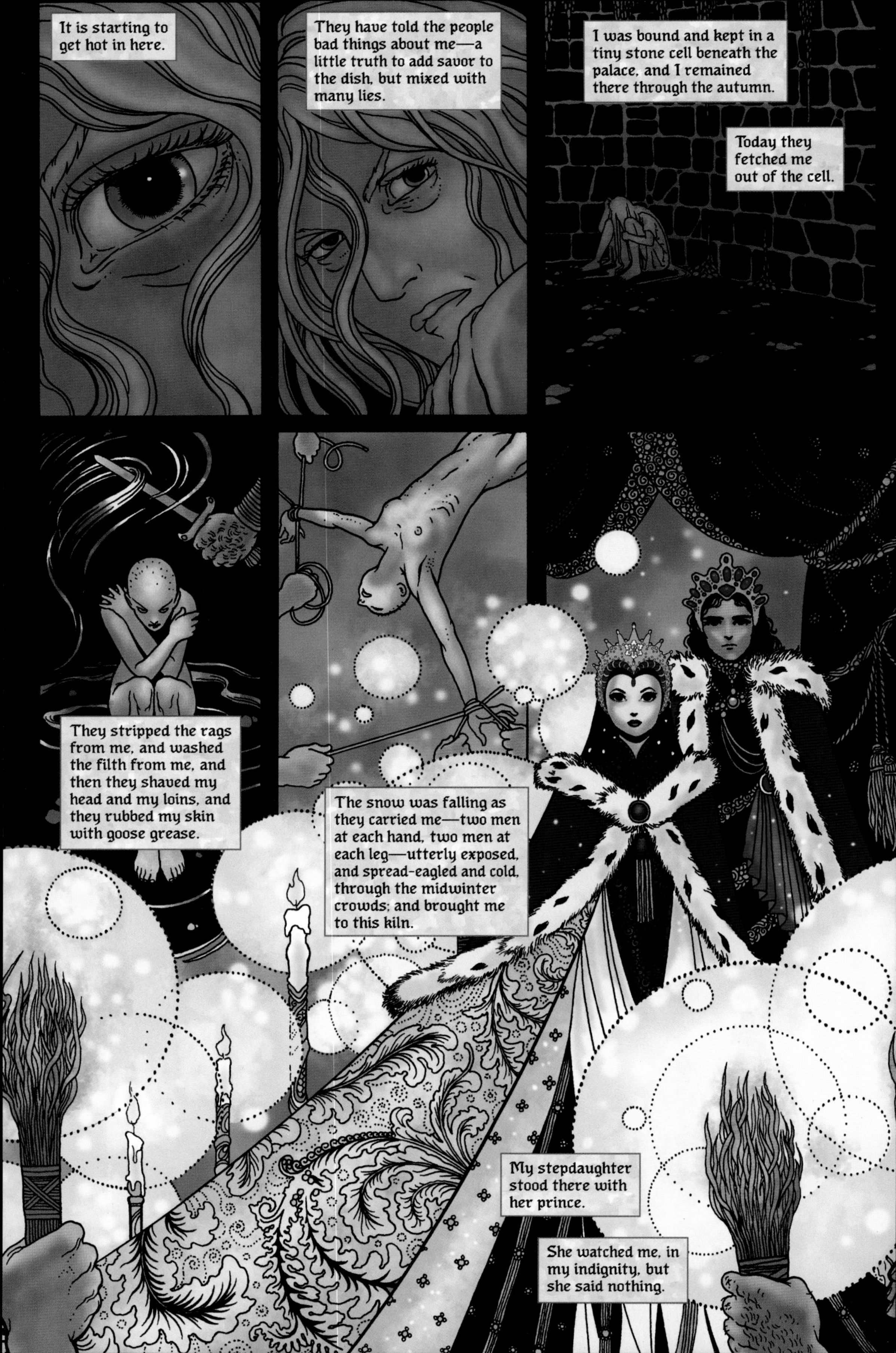
It is starting to get hot in here.
They have told the people bad things about me—a little truth to add savor to the dish, but mixed with many lies.
I was bound and kept in a tiny stone cell beneath the palace, and I remained there through the autumn.
Today they fetched me out of the cell.
They stripped the rags from me, and washed the filth from me, and then they shaved my head and my loins, and they rubbed my skin with goose grease.
The snow was falling as they carried me—two men at each hand, two men at each leg—utterly exposed, and spread-eagled and cold, through the midwinter crowds; and brought me to this kiln.
My stepdaughter stood there with her prince.
She watched me, in my indignity, but she said nothing.

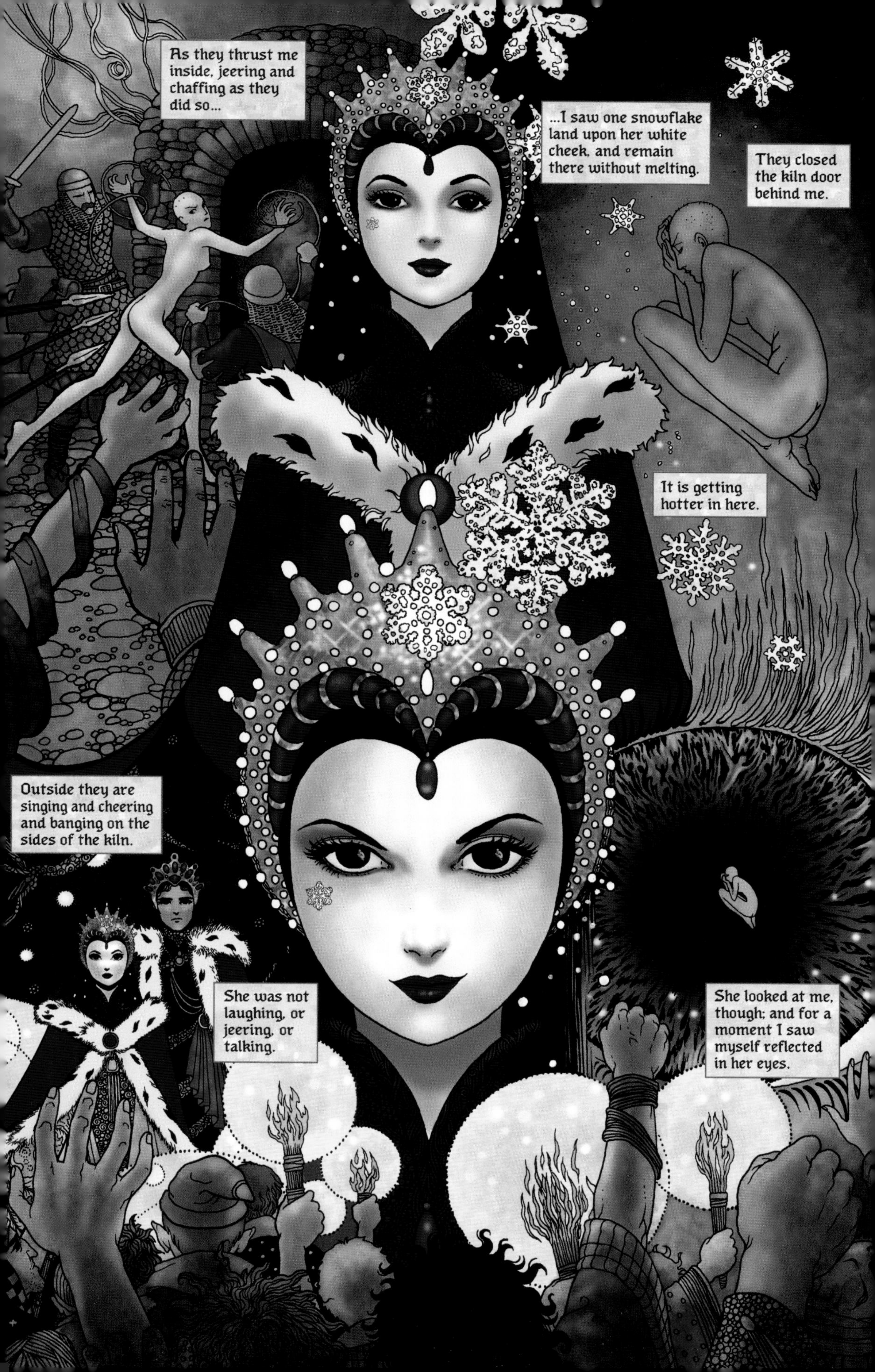
As they thrust me inside, jeering and chaffing as they did so...
...I saw one snowflake land upon her white cheek, and remain there without melting.
They closed the kiln door behind me.
It is getting hotter in here.
Outside they are singing and cheering and banging on the sides of the kiln.
She was not laughing, or jeering, or talking.
She looked at me, though; and for a moment I saw myself reflected in her eyes.

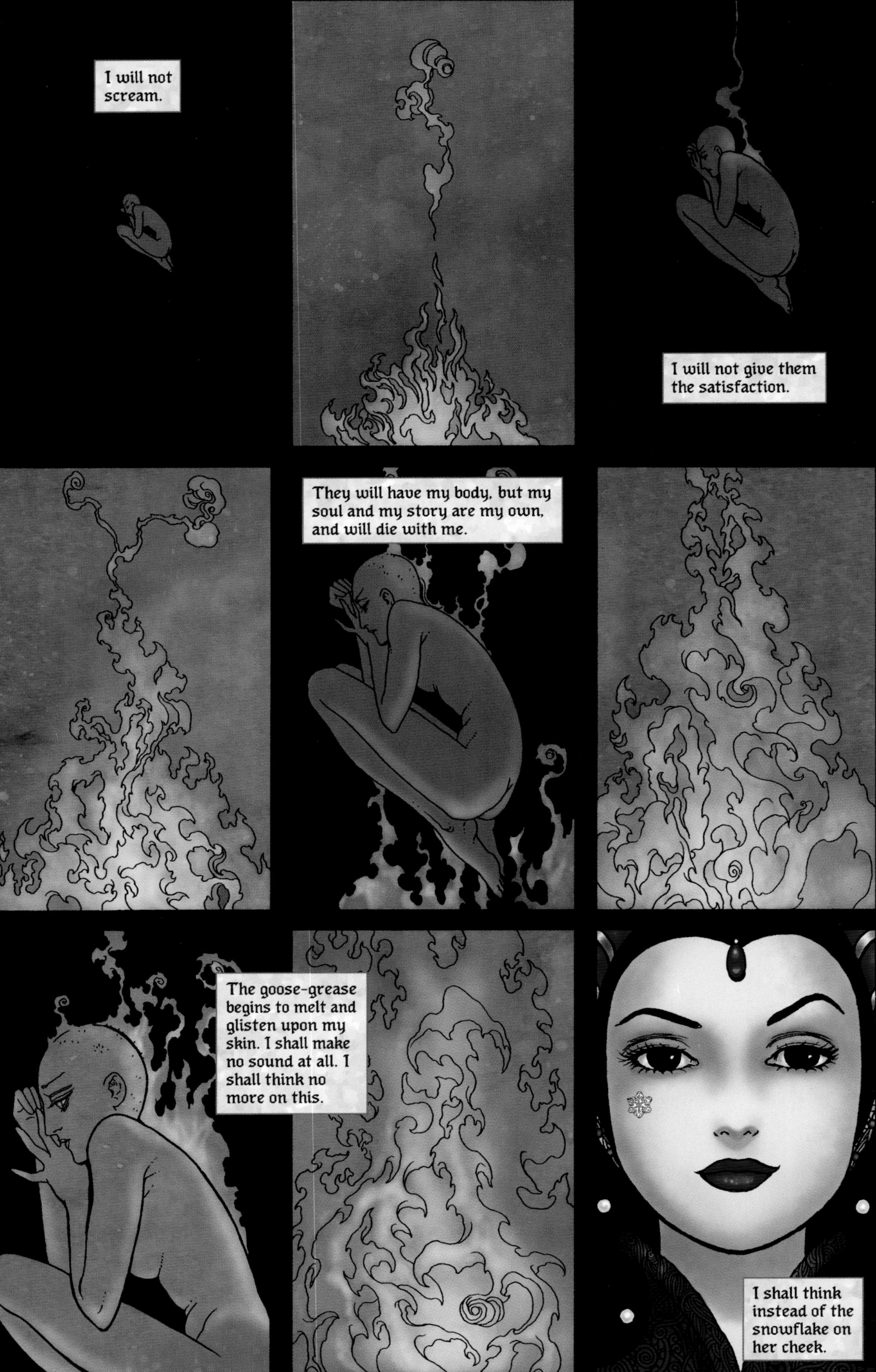
I will not scream.
I will not give them the satisfaction.
They will have my body, but my soul and my story are my own, and will die with me.
The goose-grease begins to melt and glisten upon my skin. I shall make no sound at all. I shall think no more on this.
I shall think instead of the snowflake on her cheek.

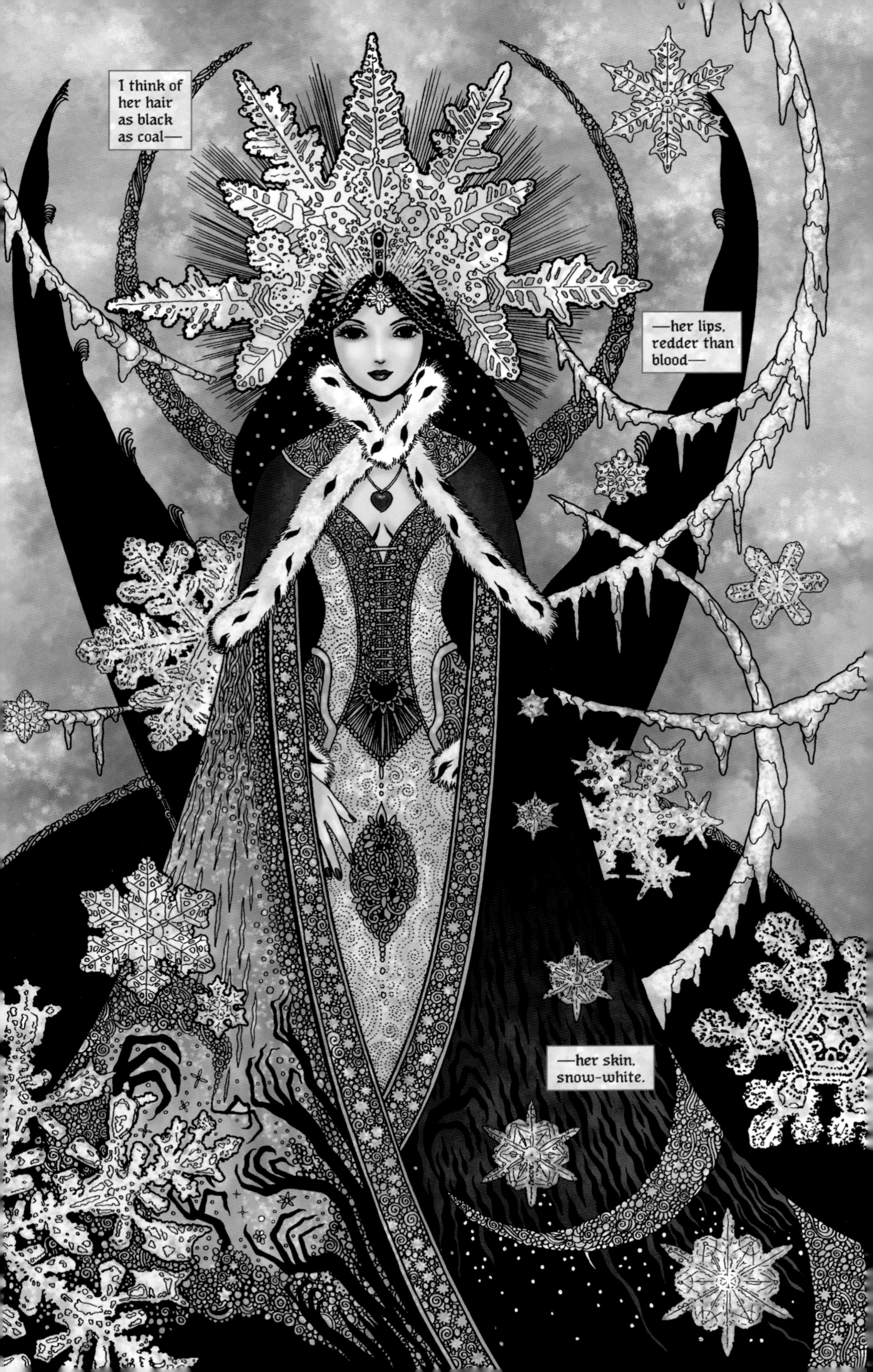
I think of her hair as black as coal—
—her lips, redder than blood—
—her skin, snow-white.

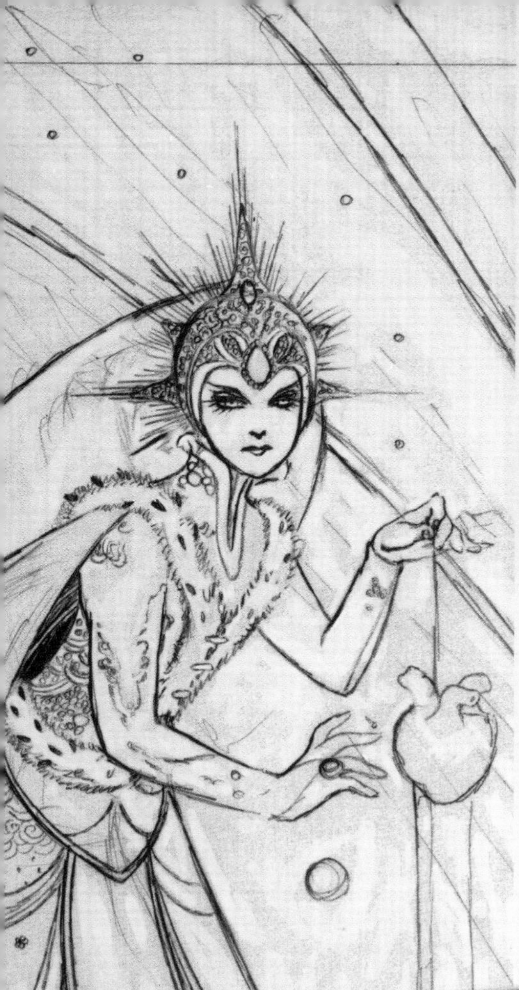

SNOW, GLASS, APPLES™

Notes by
COLLEEN DORAN

I've admired Harry Clarke's work since I was a teenager. I mistook his drawing *An Angel of Peace* for art by Aubrey Beardsley, then spent years trying to track down information about his life and creations. He became a major influence on my work, but there wasn't much enthusiasm for this highly decorative style when I first got into comics, so I didn't get much opportunity to go as far as I wanted with this look.

Neil Gaiman, also a great admirer of Clarke, decided that *Snow, Glass, Apples* would be a great story for this style.

Here you see early cover designs and sketches. I wish I'd been able to complete that second sketch as well as the final! Maybe I'll finish it later, just for kicks.

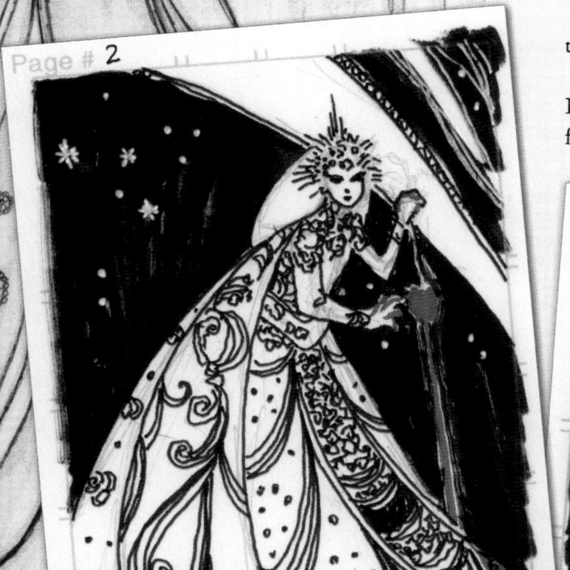
Page # 2

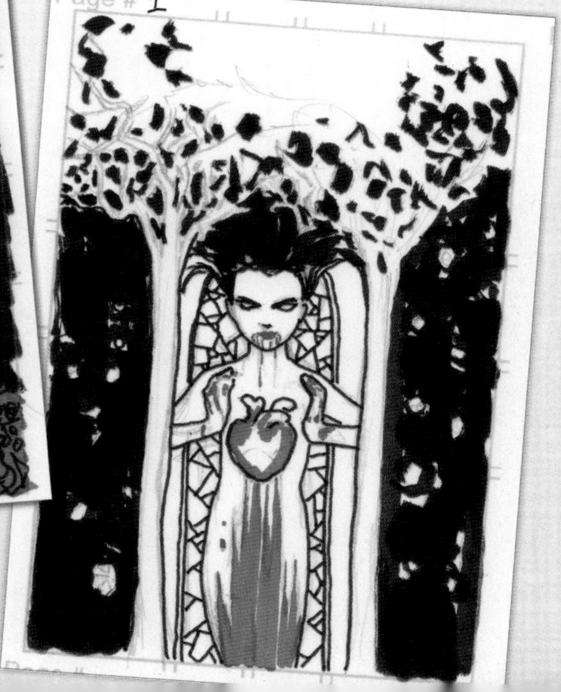
Page # 1

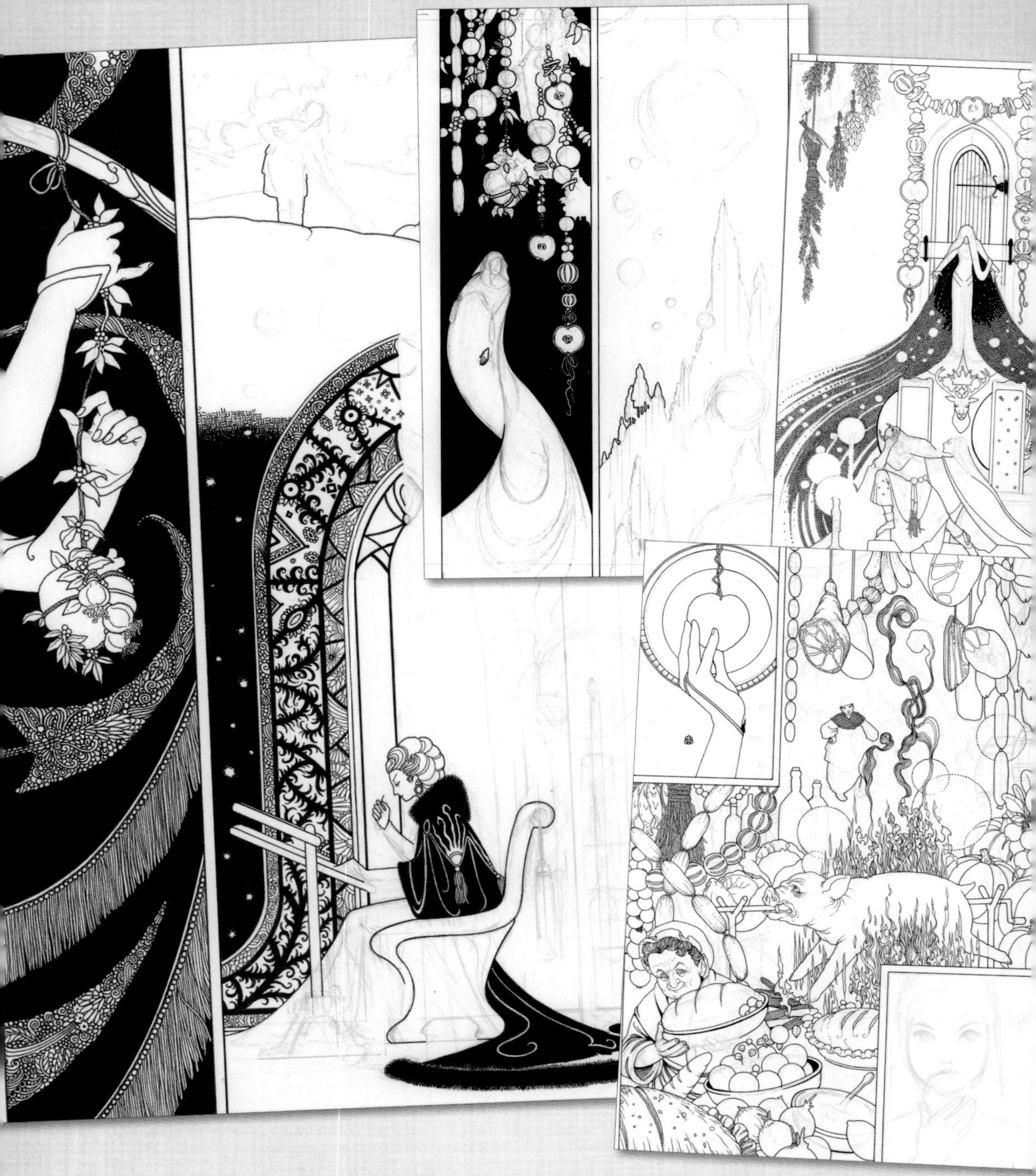

To the right, another unused cover sketch, which Neil wisely decided looked too much like a young-adult novel. We didn't want this book to appeal to kids, for obvious reasons.

On this page, scans of the art in progress. Most of the art on this book was done entirely by hand, including all the niggling little details and heavy blacks. As you may imagine, this is an exceptionally labor-intensive approach.

The kitchen scene was one of my favorites to draw. My coloring assistant Val Trullinger, with whom I worked on *Amazing Fantastic Incredible Stan Lee*, ended up doing much of the color on this page. However, I decided it would be safest to have Val help out with flats but do the rest of the final color myself because it was too hard to match coloring styles. I ended up repainting everything, even my own flats, which I'd botched at one point. Since this is my first major project coloring line art, and I'd never worked with a flatter before, her technical assistance was a huge help.

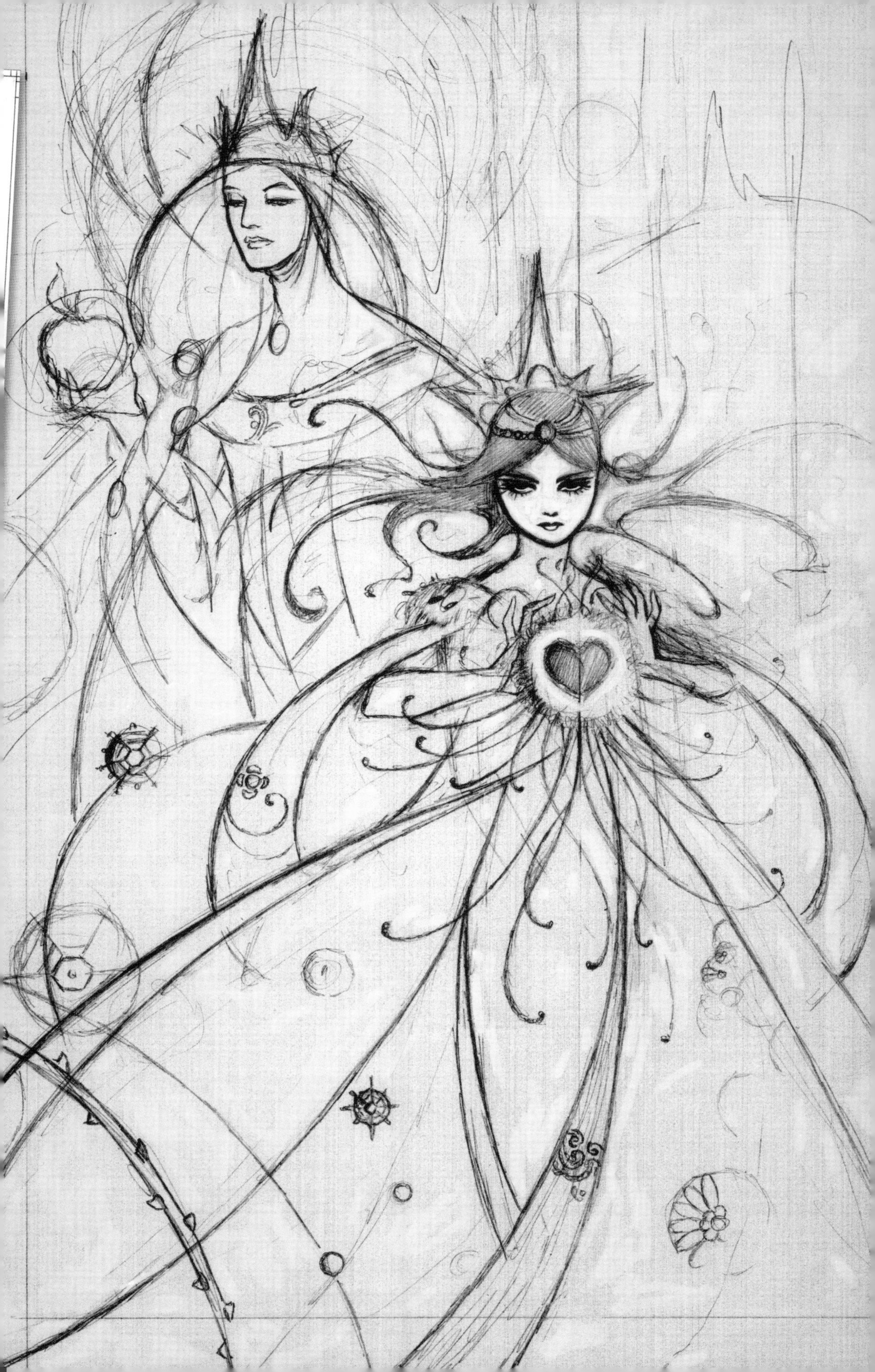

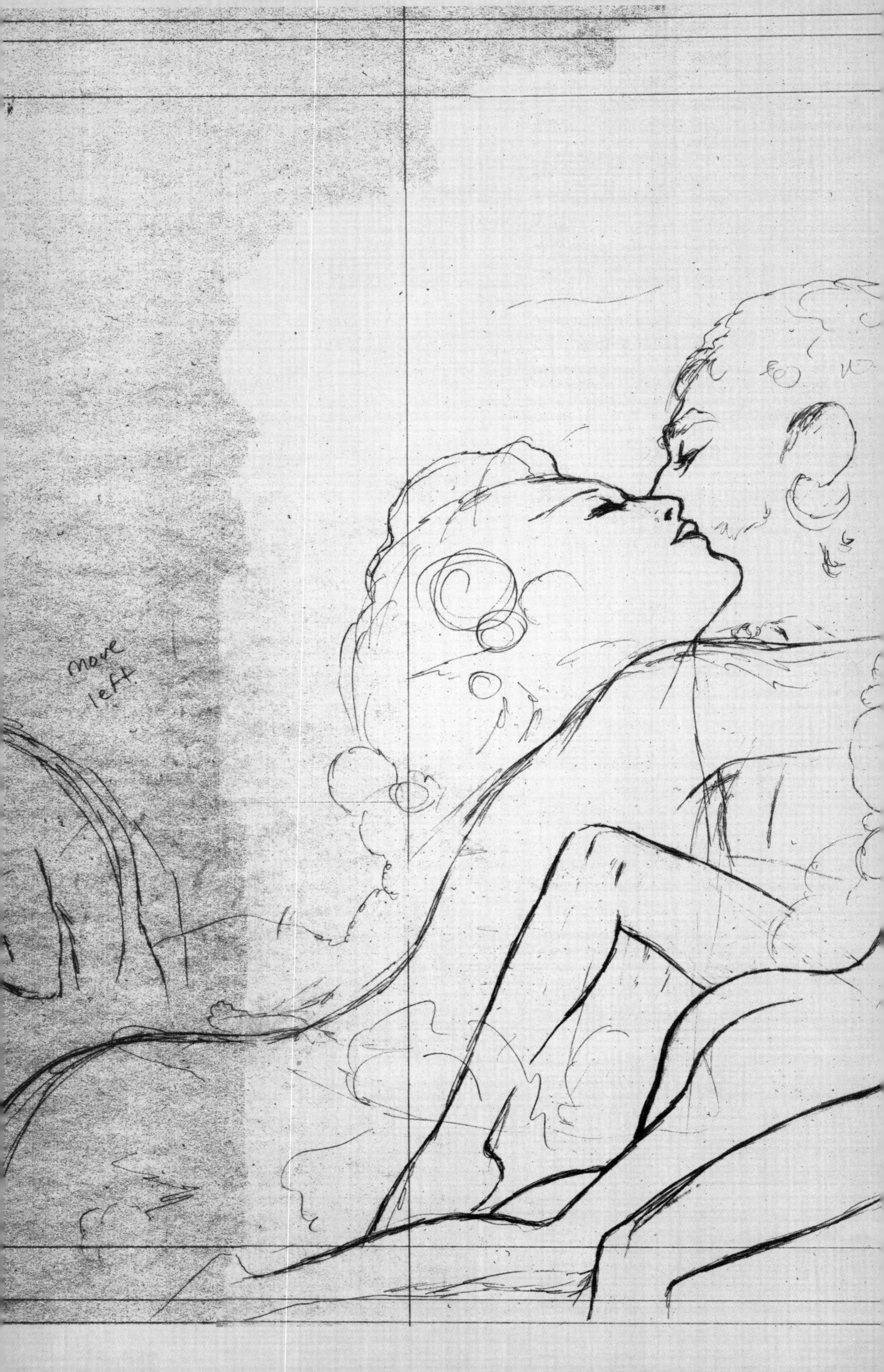
move left

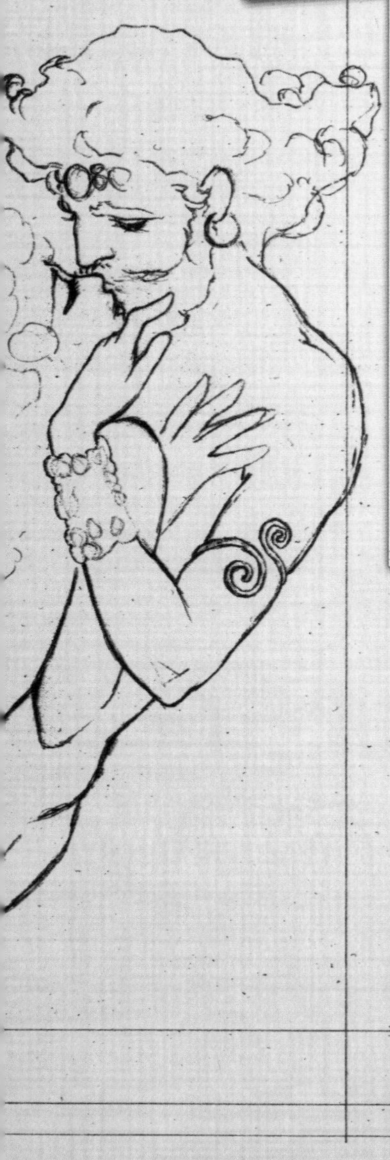
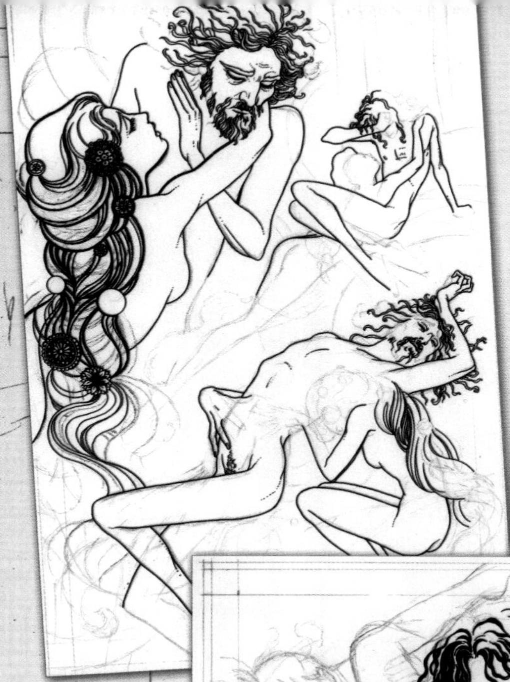
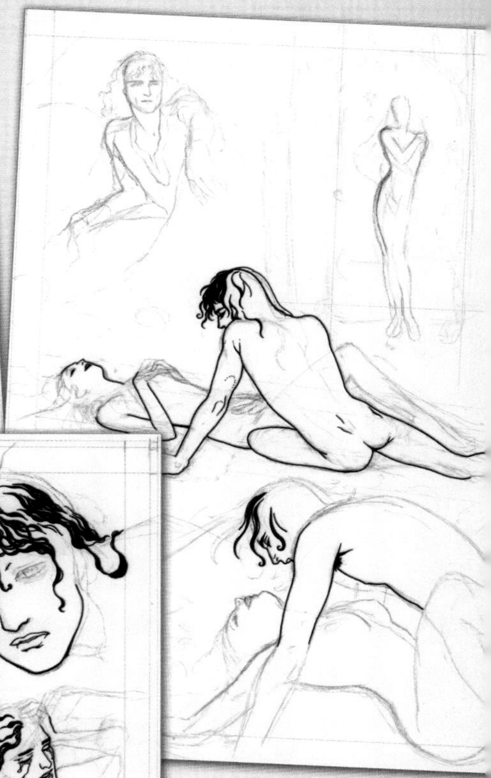
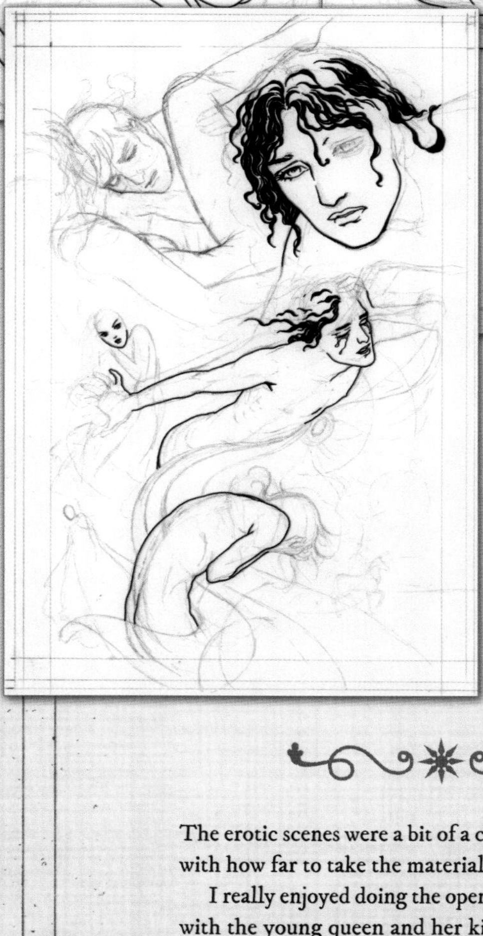

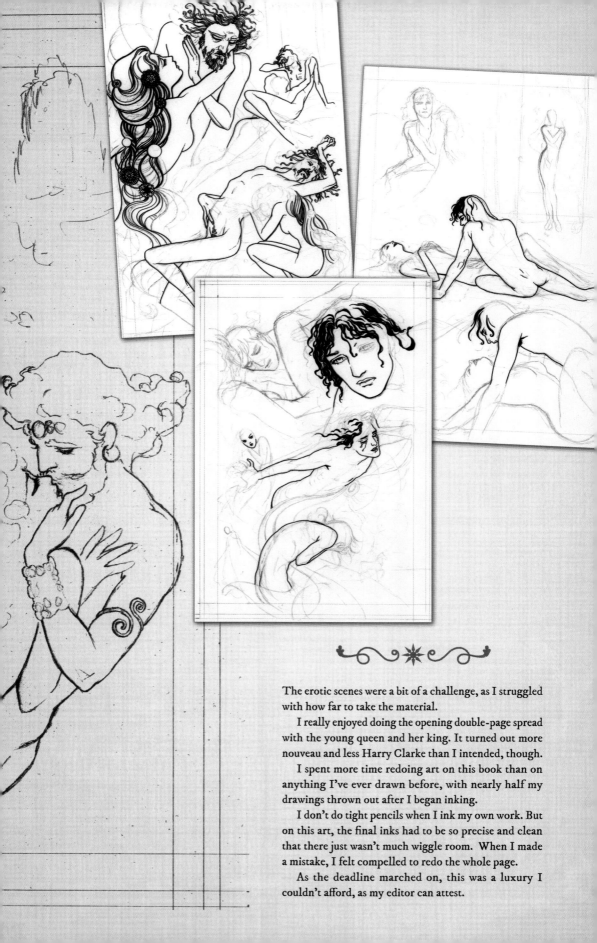

The erotic scenes were a bit of a challenge, as I struggled with how far to take the material.

I really enjoyed doing the opening double-page spread with the young queen and her king. It turned out more nouveau and less Harry Clarke than I intended, though.

I spent more time redoing art on this book than on anything I've ever drawn before, with nearly half my drawings thrown out after I began inking.

I don't do tight pencils when I ink my own work. But on this art, the final inks had to be so precise and clean that there just wasn't much wiggle room. When I made a mistake, I felt compelled to redo the whole page.

As the deadline marched on, this was a luxury I couldn't afford, as my editor can attest.

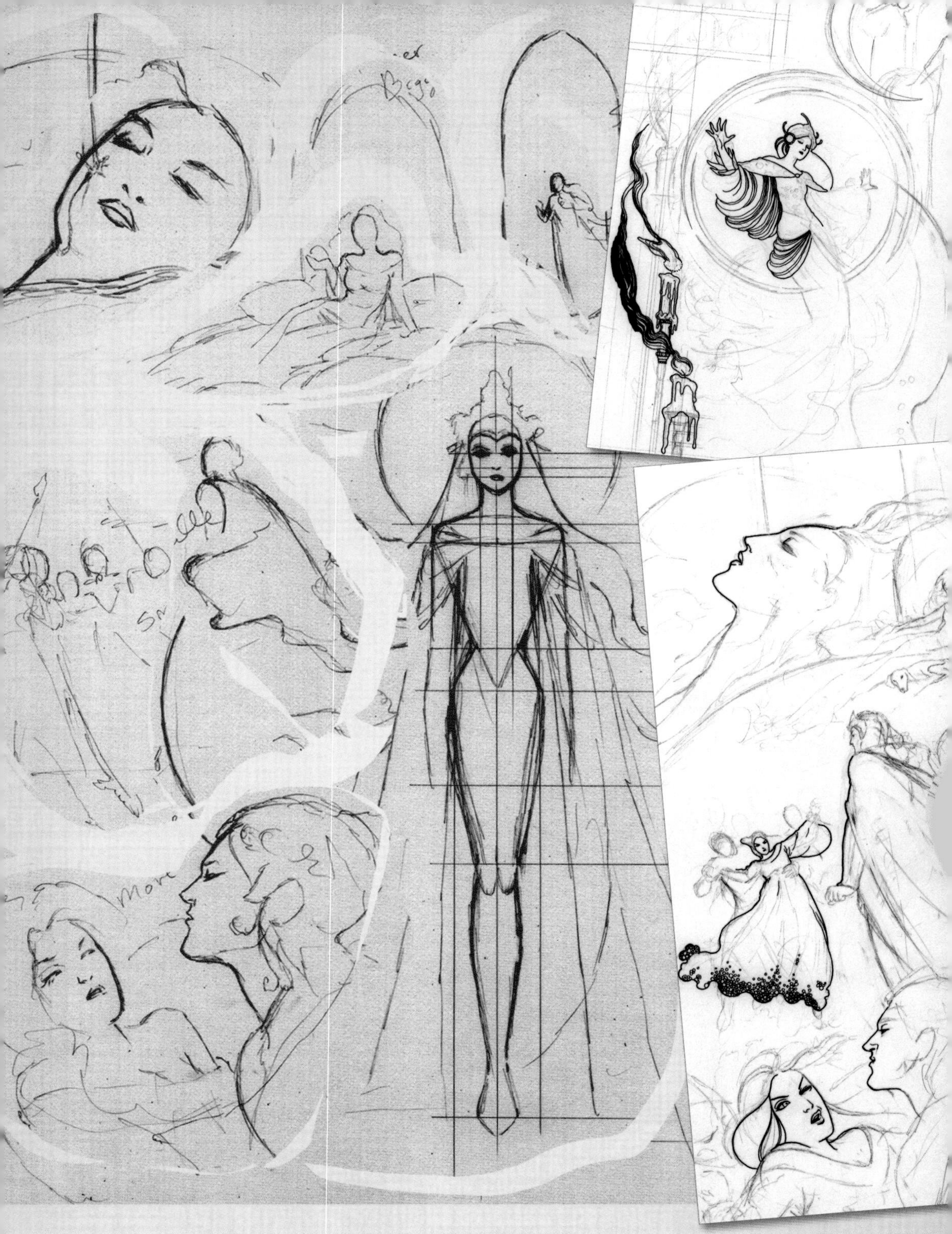

I did three versions of this page as Snow White confronts the queen. I took my original sketches, scanned them, then cut and pasted elements on the computer to work out the final composition.

The manga-looking eyes you see here are based on Clarke's style.

Over the years people assume I adopted this look into my comic art from manga, but the *fin de siècle*–era artists, creators like Beardsley and Clarke, were my early influences long before I'd ever

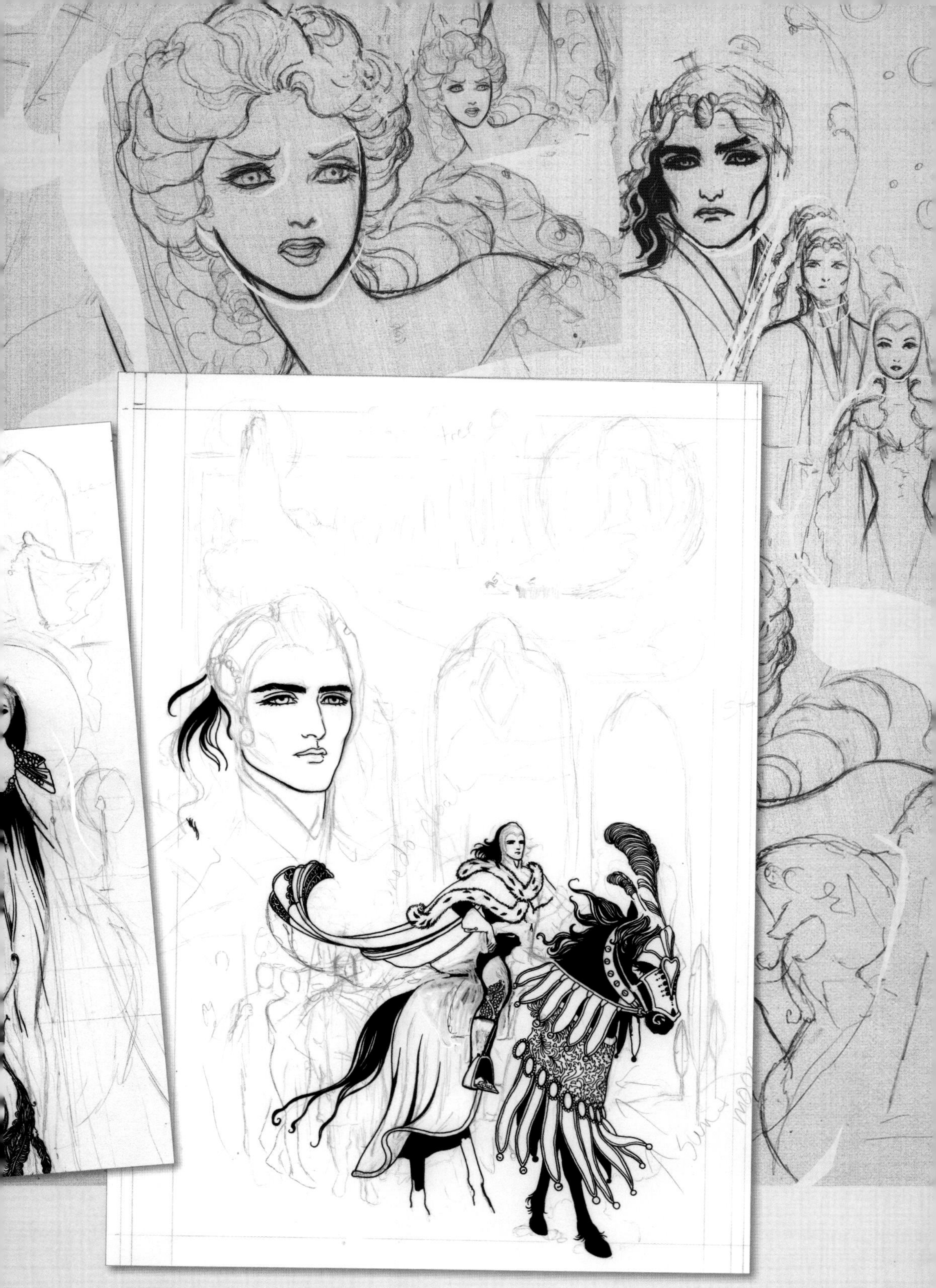

seen manga. Clarke's work predates the manga big-eye affectation, though I'm sure I was predisposed to liking manga art because of my exposure to Beardsley and Clarke.

Clarke's approach to the human figure is very attenuated and affected, and I didn't want it to dominate the feel of the book. Still, I went with a more stylized look than I usually do.

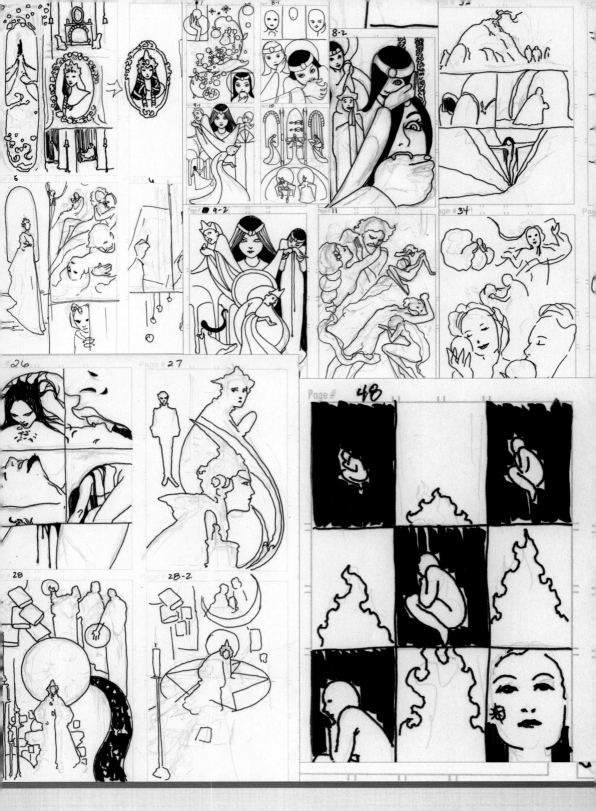

I strictly limited panel borders and used page flow to indicate the passage of time, mood, and feeling. For moments that require time beats, as on page 48, I used panel borders.

Most of the story is told from inside the queen's head, so I wanted a free-flowing sensibility. The challenge is to keep the narrative moving without confusing the reader or the poor letterer, who needs to be very careful with his word balloon placement.

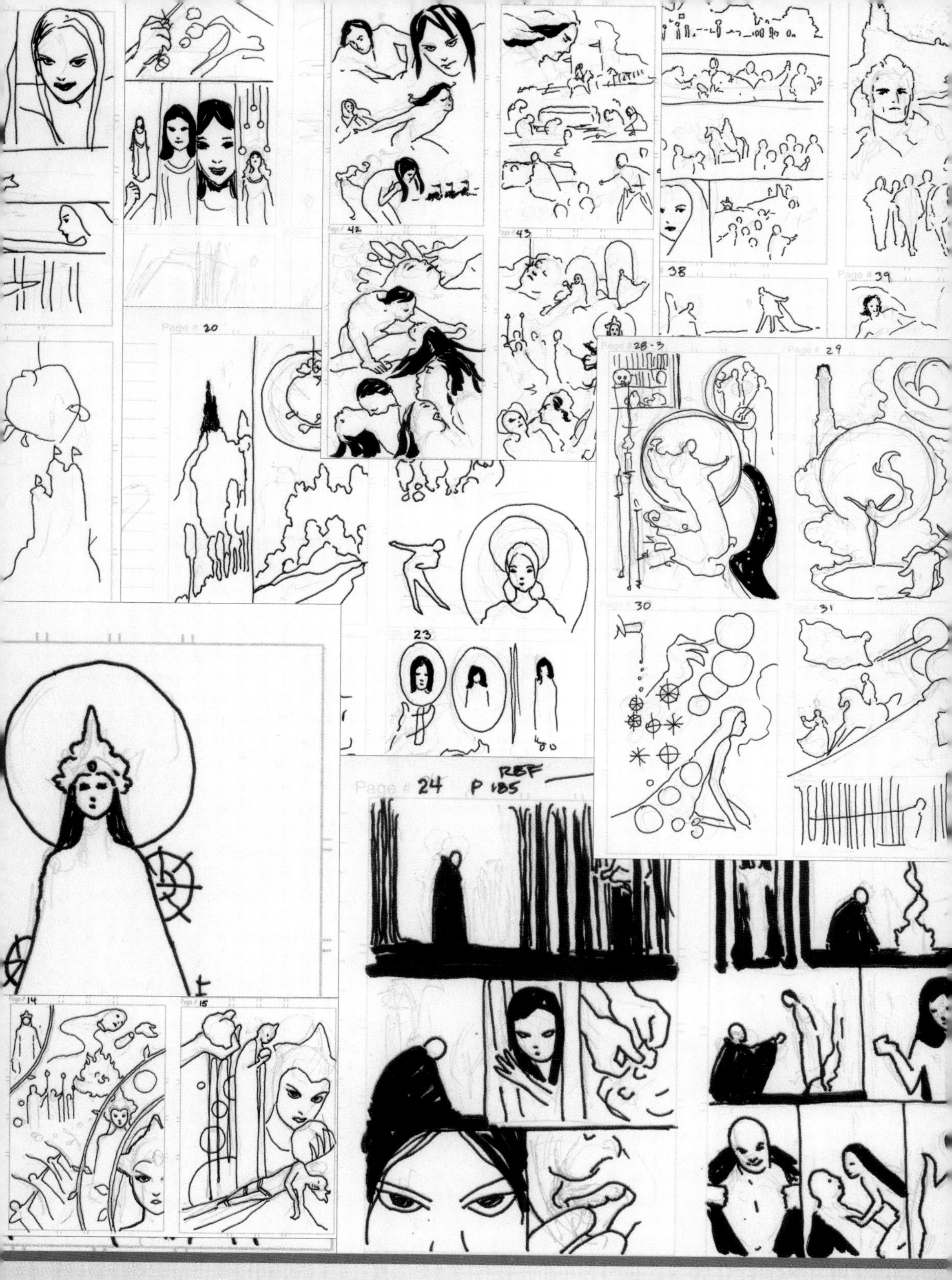

Page # 20
Page # 42
Page # 43
38
Page # 39
Page # 28-3
Page # 29
Page # 30
Page # 31
23
Page # 24
REF
P 185
Page # 14
Page # 15

For final pencils, I scanned the thumbnails, which are only about two inches high, blew them up to the final page size of about 9″x 13″, and using a lightbox, traced the thumbnails onto a sheet of Bristol board. This helps to preserve the energy of the original sketch.

I love being able to work out composition problems on the computer, which can save hours of drawing and redrawing. However, all of my final art is entirely by hand, and I don't do "blue-line pencils" as many artists do.

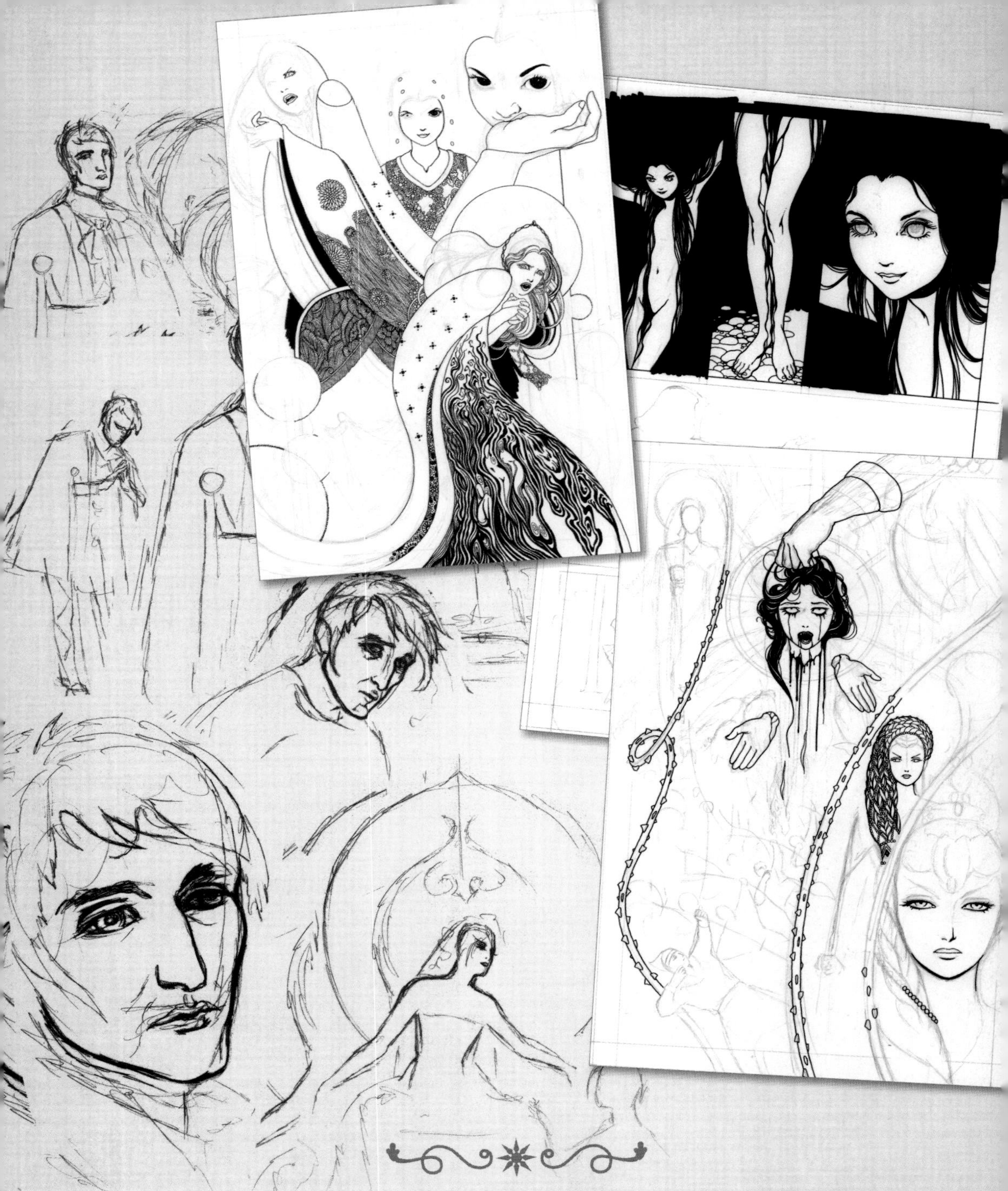

The Fair Lord is based on two works by Clarke: the main figure in *The Mad Mulrannies*, Clarke's illustration for JM Synge's *The Playboy of the Western World*, and his stained-glass work, *The Song of the Mad Prince*. *The Mad Mulrannies* was also the basis for the art on page 18. Other references from Clarke's art include illustrations from Poe's *The Pit and the Pendulum*, and a tiny spot illustration of two stylized horses ended up being incorporated into the queen's embroidery.

Clarke was the leader of the Irish Arts and Crafts Movement, and is probably best known for his stained glass. Since I'd only ever seen old, faded reproductions of his illustrations, Neil encouraged me to seek out his dazzling color originals. I went to Dublin, Ireland to get photos and reproductions of many of Clarke's works featuring deep, jewel-like blues, which I incorporated into my color approach, though my work is far more restrained than Clarke's.

I'm deeply grateful to Neil, our editor Daniel Chabon, and Dark Horse for giving me this great opportunity and so much creative freedom on this book.